JOSH

Possessing the Land

Albert McShane

JOHN RITCHIE
CHRISTIAN PUBLICATIONS

40 BEANSBURN, KILMARNOCK, SCOTLAND

ISBN 0 946351 40 6

Copyright © 1994 John Ritchie Ltd
40 Beansburn, Kilmarnock, Scotland

Front Cover
View looking north towards Hazor from a cliff-top on the west side of the Sea of Galilee. Joshua travelled this way en route to fight the king of Hazor and his allies (see Joshua 11.1-20). Joshua later allocated this territory to Naphtali, the most northerly of the tribal allocations (see Joshua 19).

Photograph kindly supplied by Cyril E Hocking, esq..

Typeset by EM-DEE Productions
Glasgow. 041 427 7846
Printed by Bell & Bain Ltd., Glasgow

Contents

DIVIDING THE LAND

ENJOYING THE LAND

Joshua:
Possessing the Land

INTRODUCTION

The Book of Joshua is perhaps the most encouraging book in the OT, for it records the success story of Israel's conquest of Canaan. At no other time in the Nation's history was there so little failure, and so little complaining amongst its people. Unlike Samuel and some other books in Scripture, it is true to its title, for throughout its pages the man Joshua is ever to the forefront. Admittedly, the period covered by it is short - less than thirty years in all. When we take into account the gap between chs. 22 and 23, which must have been about twenty years, the history recorded in detail in it cannot be longer than seven years, nevertheless, it would be difficult to find anywhere in history an account of so much accomplished in so short a time. For two or three million people to invade a fortified Land, where the cities were surrounded by massive walls, defended by giants as well as ordinary soldiers; to conquer it, and to establish themselves in it, was an achievement second to none. The wonder of this miracle is increased, when we remember that this was all accomplished in such a brief period. The Land occupied was comparatively small - not more than the size of two or three counties in England so the problem of distributing it amongst so many, and satisfying them with their different lots, must have been formidable.

In order to accomplish this wonderful feat, and that

by a people who were wanderers in the wilderness and not warriors trained in the battle field, there must have been some super-power involved. We are left in no doubt about the secret of their success, for it is manifest that it was the good hand of God upon them. Whether we look at the parting of the waters, the fall of Jericho, or the standing still of the sun, we are made aware of His almighty power in action. The critics may deny that there was anything miraculous in the story, but there is a much greater difficulty in believing that the Land was conquered by such a people in their own strength, than in believing that their success was due to divine intervention.

There are four main sections in the book. After a brief introduction of nine verses, the first five chapters have to do with moving into the Land, the next six chapters deal with the wars fought to capture it, chs. 12 to 22 tell us how the conquered Land was distributed amongst the tribes, and the closing two chapters, are an epilogue. It begins with the death of Moses, and ends with the death of Joshua. Interspersed in its pages are matters which interrupt the success story, but these are, nevertheless, closely connected to it, such as the sin of Achan ch. 7, the stratagem of the Gibeonites ch. 9, and the setting up of the altar Ed ch. 22.

An attempt has been made to view Joshua as an appendix to Deuteronomy, and to speak of the hexateuch instead of the pentateuch, but while it does carry on the story after the death of Moses, by no means can it be seen as having the legislative character of the former writing. We must look at this book as forming the foundation of the historical books of the Old Testament. These history books continue until Nehemiah, for in it we have the last date given us in the Nation's OT chronology. The period covered in its history between Joshua and Nehemiah is about a millennium. We know there will be another millennium in the future, when again the Nation will play a leading role, but with the true King upon the Throne, the history of it will be a very different story.

The chronology of the brief period recorded in Joshua is all but impossible to decide in detail. The short account of the interview which Caleb had with Joshua, given in ch. 14 in which he says that he was forty years old when he spied out the Land, is perhaps the most helpful statistic we have. If thirty eight years more were spent in the wilderness this means that when he entered the Land he was seventy eight and when the wars were over he had reached the ripe age of eighty five. From this we can learn that the initial wars lasted seven years, but it is the next period that is the most difficult to settle. If we assume that Joshua was about the same age as his friend Caleb, or even a little older, he was possibly over eighty when he entered Canaan, and almost ninety when the wars were over. He died at a hundred and ten, so he was about twenty years in retirement. There is certainly a long break between chs. 22 and 23, but to say exactly how long is impossible because of the lack of information.

A further difficulty arises when we ask, "Who was the writer of the book?" Whoever he was, he makes clear that he shared in the events which are recorded in it. It could well be that Joshua kept the records himself and from these one of the elders who outlived him, completed the final details given to us in the closing chapter. If this be so, there is a parallel in the book of Deuteronomy, for Moses wrote all of that book, except the account of his death and burial which is given in the closing chapter.

Great exception has been taken to this book because it records the destruction of the previous occupiers of Canaan, the taking of their cities, and the slaughter of all that breathed. Many claim that such unrighteous actions and such cruel treatment could not possibly be sanctioned by any one who claims to be God. One thing is clear, the Israelites were not to blame, for they did not set out to go there of their own volition, but rather by the direct guidance of God. Furthermore, they could not have possessed it, as we have seen, unless the same One had enabled them. Even more strange is the fact that, instead of blaming them for dispossessing its inhabitants, the Lord blames them for failing to do so completely. Our answer to this supposed anomaly is that the God of man's imagination is not the God of the Bible. As sovereign ruler He has the duty, as well the right, to deal with men and to punish them for their sinfulness. In the Flood and in the destruction of the cities of the plain, He had already manifested His rightful power to deal directly with sinners. If He used water and fire in executing His wrath, and He did, He could equally use His people as instruments to purge the earth of those whose iniquities had filled the cup of His indignation to the brim. We must not forget when Israel sinned, after they possessed the Land, He once again showed His right to punish, even though they were His own chosen people. Indeed they were driven out of the Land, and were as severely dealt with as were the nations of Joshua's day. God claimed the Land as His possession, so He could evict the tenants when their corrupt ways could no longer be tolerated by Him. It would have been inconsistent for Him to root out the wicked nations occupying it at the time of Israel's invasion, and then to allow the new dwellers, who became equally wicked, to remain in it. In judging Israel, He used nations to carry them into captivity which were even more sinful than they, so God is not only sovereign in His judgments, but is no less sovereign in the choice of instruments He employs to execute them.

LINKS WITH OTHER SCRIPTURES

THE BOOK OF DEUTERONOMY

Its opening paragraph, which relates afresh the account of the death of Moses, turns our minds back to Deuteronomy. Indeed, there is a close relationship with this book, because we learn from it that Joshua was chosen and established as the successor of Moses. By the laying on him of the hands of his master, and by him being presented as God's choice for leadership, the people were assured that they were not left as sheep without a shepherd. It was no small comfort for the new leader to learn that the Lord would be with him as He had been with Moses. Throughout Deuteronomy great stress is put upon the importance of obedience to the word of God; likewise in Joshua, especially in its introduction, the constant meditation in the Law and careful obedience to its commands are seen to be the signposts to the royal road of prosperity.

Attention will later be drawn to the many references to it in the two closing messages of Joshua. He seems to model his farewell to the Nation on the example of Moses recorded in that book.

THE BOOK OF NEHEMIAH

There are some links between the book of Joshua and the book of Nehemiah. In the former we have a people delivered from Egypt, in the latter a people delivered from Babylon. In Joshua the spies, and later the Nation, go round the walls of Jericho, in the latter,

Nehemiah himself goes round and surveys the broken-down walls of Jerusalem. One book tells of walls falling by the good hand of the Lord, the other tells of a wall being built up by the same good hand. Of the historical books, these two cover the shortest time. About thirty years are covered by Joshua, and about twelve by Nehemiah. In both books the importance of the Law is seen; Joshua was to read it, and Nehemiah records how it was read to the people, and explained to them by Ezra. When the prayer of the priests is offered up, a distinct reference to the early success of the Nation under Joshua is mentioned (Neh 9:22-25). Just as there was an Achan in the camp who troubled Joshua, so there was a Tobiah and his associates who troubled Nehemiah.

THE EPISTLE TO THE EPHESIANS

Not a few have detected a link between Joshua and Ephesians, for in this epistle the warfare of the saints is specially mentioned. The enemies they contend with are not earthly giants, but spiritual hosts of wickedness, whose sphere of operations is in the heavenly places. In Joshua the warfare was an united effort, but in Ephesians it is personal. In Joshua it was offensive warfare, but in Ephesians it is defensive. In Joshua the inheritance has to be captured and taken, in Ephesians the inheritance is already possessed. In Joshua the enemy has to be driven out, in Ephesians he has to be kept out. In Joshua there is little or no reference to armour or equipment for battle, in Ephesians the putting on of the essential equipment is specially stressed. In Joshua, faith, power, and courage are essential for success, likewise in Ephesians we have reference to the shield of faith, the power of His might, and the standing firm.

THE EPISTLE TO THE HEBREWS

The rest into which Joshua brought the Nation of Israel is viewed in Hebrew as typical of that rest into which we believers enter by faith, and so forms a link between it and the book of Joshua. It is noticeable how often the idea of rest appears in this latter book. "the land rested from war" (11:23); "the land had rest from war" (14:15); "the Lord gave them rest round about" (21:44): "the Lord your God hath given rest unto your brethren" (22:4); "the Lord hath given rest unto Israel from all their enemies" (23:1) are a number of references which make this clear. The Lord appeared to Joshua as a man, but later claimed to be "captain of the host of the Lord" (5:14); in Hebrews the manhood of Christ is stressed, as well as His deity, and He is spoken of as the "captain of their salvation" (2:10). In Joshua's closing speech he traces the history of the Nation from the time of Abraham, until the time he was speaking; in Hebrews the triumphs of the faithful are traced from Abel to the end of the Nation. When Moses pitched the tent outside the camp, he put Joshua in charge of it, and in Hebrews we read, "Let us go forth therefore unto him without the camp, bearing his reproach" (13:13).

THE APOSTLE PETER AND JOSHUA

There are some points of similarity between these two servants of God which are worthy of notice. To begin with, both had their names changed, Joshua from "Oshea" (Num 13), and Peter from "Simon" (John 1). It was Joshua's privilege to be with Moses on Mount Sinai, which became sanctified by the manifestation of the presence of God; Peter was privileged to be with the Lord on the Holy Mount. When Moses was performing his miracles in Egypt, Joshua was a witness of those wonders; Peter was a witness of the mighty acts of the Lord, which were performed during His public ministry. Joshua was allowed to walk through the bed of the Red Sea and of the flooded Jordan; Peter saw the Lord still the storm-tossed waves, and was even allowed to walk on the troubled waters himself. The walls of Jericho falling by the power of God was an outstanding example shown to Joshua of the futility of human strongholds; and the same lesson was taught to Peter when the gates of the prison opened to him of their own accord. The walls fell to let Joshua in, and the gates opened to let Peter out. In the deliverance of Rahab, we see a Gentile family saved by Joshua; likewise Peter had the joy of seeing the household of Cornelius saved. In the camp of Israel there was a covetous man called Achan who along with his family was sentenced by Joshua, and stoned to death. In the church at Jerusalem there was also a family which was covetous, whom Peter sentenced and they were carried out dead. There are some twenty years at the end of Joshua's life of which we know nothing, and there are about twenty years at the end of Peter's life of which nothing is recorded. However at almost the end of Joshua's day he told the Nation that he was "going the way of all the earth", but before he passed on he left two messages behind him. Similarly Peter tells us that "he must put off this tabernacle", but before he does so he, too, leaves two messages, his two epistles, behind him. The sermons of Joshua stress the importance of obedience to the commandments of the Lord, and the serious consequences of apostasy. Likewise Peter's first epistle emphasises the value of obedience, and his second epistle warns of the judgment that befalls the apostate. Joshua reminded the people of the good Land they had inherited, and Peter mentions the inheritance which is incorruptible, and that fadeth not away. There was great concern in the mind of Joshua for those he was leaving behind lest they be ensnared by the evils which surrounded them, for if they copied the sins of the nations they would have a sad end. In a similar manner, Peter says of those who become entangled in the pollutions of the world, that the latter end will be worse with them than the beginning.

KEY WORDS AND THOUGHTS IN JOSHUA

Like most books this one has certain outstanding features. One of these is the stress laid upon being courageous. In ch. 1:6 we read, "Be strong and of a good courage"; in v. 7 "Be thou strong and very courageous"; in v. 18 "Be strong and of a good courage"; in ch. 10:25 "Be strong and of good courage"; and in ch. 23:6 "Be ye therefore very courageous". In this connection it is interesting to note that the often-repeated expression, "Mighty men of valour", is first used in this book (1:14). Another feature of the book is the stress it puts upon obedience to the word of God. In ch. 1:7 we read, "Observe to do according to all the law"; in v. 8 "This book of the law shall not depart out of thy mouth; but thou shalt meditate therein day and night, that thou mayest observe to do according to all that is written therein"; in ch. 22:5 "Take diligent heed to do the commandment and the law ... keep his commandments"; and in ch. 23:6 "To keep and to do all that is written in the book of the law of Moses".

There are certain words repeated in this book which should be noted. For example, the title given to the Ark - "The Ark of the covenant" while it is used by other writers but seldom here it occurs thirteen times. The importance of the valleys also appears, so we read of "valley" twenty six times. The word "swear" occurs some fifteen times. The points of the compass are frequently mentioned: "north" twenty five times, "south" twenty nine times, "east" twenty two times, but strangely, the "west" is mentioned only twice. As we would expect, "pass over" is frequent, some fifty three times, "ascend" or "rise up" thirty seven times, and "inheritance" forty five times. It is interesting also to notice that the idea of "meditating" in the Law is first introduced into Scripture in ch. 1:8.

In reading this success story which has for its central character a leader of the first magnitude, we ought to be able to learn some important lessons from it as to the characteristics of a true leader in God's assemblies. We could also learn how much can be accomplished by a fully-trained man even in a short space of time.

THE MAN JOSHUA

It would be most unreasonable to consider the Book of Joshua without looking closely at the man who is, throughout its pages, its central character. Joshua was a descendant of Joseph, so, unlike his master, Moses, he had Egyptian blood in his veins, for Pharaoh gave Joseph Asenath to wife, who was an Egyptian. About eight or nine generations separated the two men. His father's name was Nun which means "fish", so he is mostly called "Joshua the son of Nun". His parents named him Oshea which means "salvation", but at the time when he was appointed to be one of the spies, we learn that his name has been changed to Jehoshua which means "The Lord saves". This was later contracted to "Joshua". Whether it was changed earlier than when we learn of it, we do not know, but he is called "Joshua" from the time when he is first mentioned. The Greek equivalent to this is "Jesus", so in Heb 4 Joshua is named Jesus. Because of this close relationship between the two names many have seen in him an outstanding type of Christ. The addition "son of Nun" may suggest that there were others in Israel with the same name, so he had to be distinguished in this way from them. He was born in Egypt about eighty years after the death of Joseph, and about forty years after the birth of Moses, so his early life was spent in the rigour of Egyptian bondage. If anyone had looked at him in the brick-fields under the taskmaster's lash, he could never have imagined that such a one would distinguish himself in the battle-fields of Canaan, or have the glorious finish which he had. Whatever were the humiliations experienced by Moses when he had to leave Egypt and tend the sheep of his father-in-law, these were light compared with the hardship endured by his servant, Joshua. The great difference between the two men was that Moses knew luxury before he was humiliated, whereas Joshua was born in slavery, and in early life knew nothing of dignity or honour. How the two men became acquainted we are not told. To us it is strange that a man of another tribe, and having no close relationship, should have been chosen by Moses to be his servant. Had he not sons of his own, and why was one of them not called to help his father? Why did he not choose one from his own tribe, or from the royal tribe of Judah? These are questions we cannot answer, but, nevertheless, they arise in our minds. The plagues in Egypt, and especially the first Passover, must have remained precious memories to Joshua. Likewise the parting of the waters of the Red Sea and the destruction of the mighty army of Pharaoh could not have failed to impress upon his mind the wonders of God's power. Little did he then think that one day he himself would witness and personally experience another demonstration of that same power when once again waters would be divided. Could he ever forget the sound of the loud strains, as the many thousands of Israel sang of the triumphs of the Lord? Likewise it was his lot to witness, no doubt with amazement, the first occasion when the manna fell, which was to be his own and the Nation's food for forty years.

It is one thing to be a spectator watching the power of God being demonstrated, it is quite another to be the instrument through whom it works. Not long after the crossing of the Sea the Amalekites made an attack upon Israel which resulted in sad consequences, especially for the weak and hindermost of the camp. Like most crises, this brought into the limelight the man for the hour. Neither Moses, who was a man mighty in word and deed, nor his brother Aaron, who was his assistant, made any attempt to muster the army or lead the defence forces against the assaulting foe, but the hitherto unknown man, Joshua, was entrusted with this heavy task. Without any explanation he is thus introduced to us in the Scriptures, and as the one chosen by Moses to gather the army and fight the enemy. There must have been qualities in this young man which were apparent to his master, otherwise he would not have been thrust into such a responsible and perilous position. How he learned the art of warfare is hard to say, and how he managed to lead men, some of whom were much older than himself, into that first encounter with a formidable enemy. Of this we are sure, there is no relationship between making bricks and marshalling battalions.

The war was no walk over, for there were times when the enemy seemed to be gaining the upper hand, and the whole day was spent before the issue was decided, and before Israel had won the victory. He was possibly between forty and forty five years old at this time, and is called by his aged master a "young man". In spite of his age and previous obscurity, this battle, which he fought so successfully, established him as a potential leader in Israel, and marked him out before the people as a man of destiny. One important lesson taught him on this occasion, and one which must have remained with him for the rest of his life, was that neither he nor his army could boast of their achievement. The victory was entirely due to the lifted rod in the hand of Moses, who interceded with the Lord on the mount, and obtained His help for the vital struggle transpiring in the valley below. In reality the battle was between Amalek and the Lord, so the outcome was not in doubt, still, it is not unknown for those engaged as mere instruments to imagine the victory was won by them, and thus unjustly claim the honour due to God alone. Though it never entered the mind of Joshua at this time, this encounter with Amalek was giving him a foretaste of what he would do later with the nations of Canaan.

The next important experience in the life of Joshua was when he accompanied Moses on the Mount at the giving of the Law. The elders of Israel ascended part way up where they met with, and feasted with the Lord, but he went to the top, and remained during the 40 days alone with his master. No other man in Israel was allowed to be so near to the thunderings and lightning which accompanied the presence of the Lord at that time, and which made even Moses fear and quake. If the war with Amalek taught him something of the power of God, this awful experience taught him to reverence and fear Him. It was no small test of his patience to stay on that mount, and as far as we know to have neither food nor rest during this period.

It would appear that when Moses descended the Mount and witnessed the shameful scenes around the golden calf, Joshua was with him. Later, when he pitched his tent outside the camp, he put him in charge of it. While resting in this tent, and no doubt pondering over the lonely and trying forty days he had spent on the top of Sinai, he must have been thankful that in fulfilling his duty there he was saved from being involved in the shameful idolatry, and also that he was not the servant of Aaron, nor his helper in the making of the golden calf.

Joshua was such a devoted servant to Moses that he could not tolerate anyone who would treat his master with disrespect. When two of the seventy men, who were allowed to share the Spirit's power which formerly was exclusively the portion of Moses, refused to come out to him and prophesy with the rest, but remained in the camp and prophesied there, this was more than Joshua could bear, so he enjoined upon his master to silence them. On this occasion, however, he allowed his zeal to exceed what was desired or expected, for the aged leader was not smitten with envy, nor was he the slightest perturbed at what had happened. The lesson taught Joshua at this time is an important one, for it demonstrated to him the fact, that truly great men never need to defend their own dignity.

After a period of about two years in the wilderness, the children of Israel reached the borders of the Land which they had been promised, and which they had set out to inherit. The Lord at that time directed Moses to send spies to inspect the Land, and to report to the people their findings. Among those appointed to this responsibility was Joshua, who represented the tribe of Ephraim.

The thrill and excitement of traversing the Land of Canaan and of walking in the steps of the Patriarchs must have touched the deepest emotions of Joshua's heart. The season for viewing it could not have been more opportune, for it was at the time when the grapes were ripe. The many vineyards, laden with precious fruit, must have been an attractive and appetising sight. Certainly nothing like it had been seen by him in the wilderness, nor indeed in Egypt. Which two of the twelve spies cut down the huge bunch of grapes and carried it on a pole to show to the people, we do not know, but their precious burden was ample proof that the Land they had traversed was indeed a Land of wine.

Alas, ten of the twelve spies, though compelled to admit that the Land was most fruitful, brought back an evil report of it, because their minds were filled with thoughts of its high walls and giants. Their unbelief and heartlessness was soon spread amongst the people, who, instead of rejoicing at the prospect of going over and possessing such a wonderful Land, sat down in despair and wept; nothing that either Caleb or Joshua said could change their minds, or cause them to turn to God for His help. The crisis became so serious for these two faithful witnesses, that they both were in danger of losing their lives, for the people threatened to stone them. While Caleb was the spokesman who defended faithfully the cause, and dared to differ from the majority, yet he had not to stand alone, but was nobly supported by Joshua. God honoured these men for their faithfulness, for both were given assurance by Him that they would enter the Land. Whatever other lessons Joshua may have learned at this time, one was sure and certain, namely, that it pays to take sides with God, even though the majority are opposed.

Because the Nation refused to go into the Land in dependence upon God, it was sentenced to spend thirty eight years wandering in the wilderness, during which time those who were numbered as fit for war were destroyed. It is all but impossible for us to grasp the weariness and drudgery experienced by Joshua during this long period in the wilderness. It is sad to think that the best period of his life was spent marking time with those who refused to heed his advice. Through no fault of his own, more than a third of his lifetime was wasted in wanderings. The many funerals he attended, and the heart-aches he witnessed, must have left him at times feeling depressed. There is no mention of him during these years, so like Moses before him, he lived in obscurity until he was an old man. However, when he had patiently endured, he at length saw fulfilled the promise which the Lord had given him, and for which he had longed.

When it became apparent to Moses that he would have to relinquish his responsibilities he was rightly concerned about who would take his place. The Lord made clear to him that Joshua was the one fitted for the task. In order to make this apparent to the Nation, he was directed by the Lord to arrange that the congregation be gathered together, along with Eleazar the priest, and that Joshua be formally appointed by the laying on of his hands. In this ceremony, some of the spiritual power peculiar to Moses was conveyed to his servant, and this, together with the solemn charge delivered, fitted Joshua and fully furnished him for the great work which lay before him. Thus we read of him, "And Joshua the son of Nun was full of the spirit of wisdom; for Moses had laid his hands upon him" (Deut 34:9). One cannot fail to see in these words a close parallel to Paul and Timothy.

This brief sketch of his life, up to the time when he led the Nation into the promised Land will suffice in bringing us to appreciate the man whose exploits we will follow as we make our way through the book called by his name. As we do so, more of his virtues will appear, and more of the problems he overcame will be considered.

JOSHUA AND MOSES COMPARED AND CONTRASTED

Scripture makes clear that there was never a man like Moses, either before or after him, so when he was made, the mould was broken; nevertheless, there are some of his features and experiences which, in measure, were shared by his servant, Joshua. For example, both shared the title "servant of the Lord". Moses was forty years old when he fled from Egypt, and Joshua was in his forties when he too left Egypt. Moses spent forty years of his life in the desert minding sheep, and Joshua spent forty years of his life in the wilderness. Moses did his greatest work in his eighties, so too did Joshua. God granted Moses a foretaste of his triumph over Egypt when he slew the Egyptian and hid his body in the sand, likewise, Joshua had a foretaste of his victories in Canaan when he defeated Amalek. When Moses was about to confront Pharaoh he was granted the wonderful revelation of God at the bush, and when Joshua was about to conquer the Canaanites he was given a revelation of the Lord at Gilgal. Moses learned that the Lord had come down to deliver Israel from the furnace of Egypt, and Joshua learned that the Lord was come to fight with his enemies, and was well able to defeat them seeing He was the Lord of hosts. Both men were told to remove their shoes in the holy presence of the Lord. All Israel saw the waters of the Red Sea divided for Moses to lead them through on dry ground, and all Israel saw the waters of the Jordan divided to allow Joshua to lead them into the Land. When the battle with Amalek was over, Moses built an altar and offered sacrifices to the Lord, likewise when the battle at Ai was over, Joshua built an altar of whole stones and offered burnt-offerings and peace-offerings upon it.

When we see these two men at almost the end of their lives, we notice quite a similarity about their behaviour. Both had a deep concern about the future of the Nation, and especially who would lead it when they were gone. Unlike the kings, though both men had sons, yet neither of them appointed one of these as his successor. The man who took over from Moses was highly successful, and the men who followed Joshua were also most worthy leaders. Just as Moses assembled all Israel to hear a parting message, so too did Joshua gather them to hear his parting speech. There are many links between the song of Moses in Deut 32 and the parting messages of Joshua in Josh 23 and 24. Without tracing these parallels in detail, we can mention that both leaders emphasise the might of God, and the wonder of His past doings; both recall past history to teach lessons to the new generation; and both warn the Nation of the seriousness of idolatry, and show the consequences of departure from God.

There are also many senses in which these two leaders differed. Moses was reared in a palace, but Joshua was a slave in Egypt. No one trained Moses for his post, but Joshua had at least forty years of training with his master. The powerful rod, so often used by Moses, especially when performing miracles, was never handed down to his successor. Moses brought Joshua up the Mount at the giving of the Law, but the latter was a mere bystander, while the former spoke face to face with the Lord. Even though we often read of the Lord speaking to Joshua, yet there was an intimacy with the Lord enjoyed by Moses, his master, which was unknown to him. To us it is strange that the Nation never seemed to give Joshua the trouble that it gave to Moses. The new generation must have learned their lesson from their fathers, and dreaded the punishment of rebellion. Apparently whatever Joshua said to them was heeded and obeyed without question. Moses, in spite of his plea and longing to pass over into the Land, died without having his desire gratified, while Joshua visited it as a spy, and spent the last thirty years of his life in it. Both men were buried in a mountain, yet Moses had a strange death and burial, whereas Joshua apparently died of natural causes and had a normal burial.

ENTERING THE LAND
(ch. 1:1-ch. 5:12)

THE PREFACE (1:1-9)

The first nine verses of ch. 1 give us an introduction to the book. In vv. 1-2 we have Joshua's communication from the Lord, and the command to lead the people over Jordan; in vv. 3 - 5 he is told of the compass of the Land, and is assured of its conquest; and in vv. 6 - 9 he is exhorted to be courageous, and to be careful to obey the commandments of the Lord.

Like many other books of the OT such as Exodus, Leviticus, and Numbers, the book of Joshua is connected to the one which precedes it, by the particle "now" or "and", for in a real sense it is a continuation of the story at the end of Deuteronomy. It is noticeable that Deuteronomy is not in this way connected to Numbers for the simple reason that it was written, not for sojourners in the wilderness, but for the guidance of the people when they would enter their inheritance. The news of Moses' death and burial recorded in Deut 34 was not unknown to Joshua, but is re-echoed in his ears by the Lord Himself. In what way the Lord spoke to Joshua we are not told. Whether it was through the Urim and Thummim, or from the mercy-seat, or directly, as He did to Moses, we are not sure, but the latter was the most likely, for this much is plain, there was no barrier or blockage in the lines of communication between the Lord and His servant. The loss of those who had played such a prominent part in the Nation, both while leaving Egypt, and during the forty years in the wilderness, must have caused a serious crisis, for the people must have had deep concern as to what was to happen next. Due to his failure at the Rock Moses was not allowed to lead the them into the Land, but now that he was dead the way was open, so Joshua is commanded to lead them across the Jordan into it. Because we know how wonderfully the Lord helped in this operation, we do not appreciate the magnitude and formidableness of the task assigned to him, nor do we realise how he felt when he heard of his responsibility, which was conveyed to him in a few brief words. To lead two million and more people through a flooded river, to cause them to set up their camp in a place which they had never seen before, and to settle them there for the remainder of their lives, was no small venture. Even though this was the goal aimed at from the day they left Egypt, yet when it was within reach the task to be undertaken must have been a daunting one.

When God gives command to do something difficult, He often gives promises to encourage the doers. This is what we find here, for Joshua was assured that all the Land on which he would place his foot was to be possessed. Indeed, in the purpose of God it was already in possession. He not only gives promises, but also the enablement to embrace them, nor does He give commandments without giving the needed strength to obey them. If we think of the command to the man with the withered hand, or of the command to Lazarus to come forth from the tomb, we can see that only by the power of the Lord was obedience possible. On the other hand, the responsibility for Joshua was to set his foot upon the promised possession, so he was not to sit back and find himself snugly dwelling in Canaan. In this we learn that human responsibility goes alongside divine sovereignty. The extent of the coasts of the Land is given as from the Wilderness in the south to the forest of Lebanon in the north, and from the Euphrates in the east to the Mediterranean in the west. The land of the Hittites is the same territory described by its then present inhabitants. As we have already seen the area of this territory was not large, yet it was seldom fully occupied by the Israelites, for pockets of the enemy were to be found holding on to their part of it even until the times of David. Certainly, when the time came that Joshua's leadership was near its end, "There was still much land to be possessed". In the spiritual realm in our day we all have to confess that we have not fully possessed our inheritance in Christ, even though the Holy Spirit has been given to us for the purpose of enabling us do so.

One serious obstacle in the way of Joshua and the people possessing the Land was the presence in it of giants. These mighty men terrified most of the spies, and were a force to be reckoned with. The Lord assured him that no man, be he ever so tall or strong, would be able to stand against him. Already he had witnessed an example in Moses of how the Lord, who was with him, proved more than a match for the greatest of men, for even Pharaoh, who was the most powerful man in his time, was overcome and drowned in the Red Sea.

As long as Joshua would live, he had the assurance given to him that the Lord would be with him. The promise, "I will not fail thee, nor forsake thee" is a repeat of the promise first given to Jacob, and again repeated by Moses to the people at the time when he was about to leave them (Deut 31:6). It was intended to dispel their fears and to brace up their courage as they were about to go over and conquer the Land. Later, when faced with attacks from the enemy, sometimes with their united forces, this promise was repeated to Joshua and was no small encouragement to him (see ch. 10:8; 11:6).

Mortal man is often plagued with fear and timidity, but these weaknesses must have no place in the hearts of those who fight the Lord's battles, so Joshua is told to be "strong and of a good courage" and "to be very strong and very courageous". To be otherwise would have revealed his lack of trust in God's almighty power. It is noteworthy that earlier Moses gave instructions that the faint-hearted should be allowed to return home from the battlefield, lest they should discourage others engaged in the fight (Deut 20:8). If the ordinary soldier's faintheartedness was sure to be contagious, how much more would the cowardice of the captain of the army adversely effect the morale of the entire host. Later history shows that Saul, being full of fear himself, produced fearful followers (1Sam 13:7), and contrariwise, David's courage was reproduced in his mighty men.

The courage of Joshua was not to be confined to the battlefield, but was in a special sense to be manifest in his obedience to God's word. Obviously his enjoyment of divine help in his mission was conditional on his submission to the demands of the Law. Foolhardiness, or even mere natural boldness, however successful in the battlefields of this world, would in this case be of no avail, but would lead to disastrous results. Only obedience to the commandments of the Lord would bring success. No more complete misunderstanding of God's promise at this time could have been entertained, than to imagine that it was a guarantee of His help irrespective of how the people and their leader behaved. Indeed, we all know that Joshua learned this painful lesson at his first attempt to take Ai, for Israel's sin and disobedience at that time left the people helpless before their enemies. No one can be obedient to God's word who is not acquainted with it, so he was instructed to become a diligent student of it. We might imagine it would be a loss of precious time for an army general, who had so many things demanding his attention, to sit and meditate upon the word of God, but the key to his prosperity was his humble submission to divine instructions. David taught the Nation the same lesson when he penned the words of Ps 1:1 -3. It is obvious he had this very passage in mind while writing concerning the blessed man, "his delight is in the law of the Lord; and in his law doth he meditate day and night....and whatsoever he doeth shall prosper". Joshua might have excused himself from this duty by rightfully claiming that it was the priests responsibility to teach the law, and he could safely leave it to them to do their own work; but though it was not his role to be a teacher of the people, yet it was his part to know the law in order to obey it. Alas, it has to be feared that some read the Scriptures mainly to teach others rather than to become acquainted with the mind of God revealed therein for themselves.

In reviewing this introduction to this book we shall seek to point out some valuable lessons in it for those who are called to lead God's people in this day. One of these is the change that comes when older leaders are taken away. We all know what it is to lean upon trusted men, and almost to conclude that the work of God could not proceed without them. However, those left behind have to learn that no man is indispensable, and that while revering the memories of past leaders, they are, nevertheless, to be more concerned about their own present responsibilities. The best way to show our respect for former guides, is to carry on where they left off. Another lesson for leaders in these verses is that God gives to each man his own work. Just as Joshua was not a law-giver or the architect of the Tabernacle but a captain of the Lord's host, so they may be called upon to make advances in the work of God not attempted by their predecessors. A further lesson our passage teaches is the importance of having direct communications from the Lord. Admittedly, no man at present has the experience of the Lord speaking directly to him, as had Moses and Joshua, nevertheless, the Spirit through the Scriptures can, and does speak to men in such a clear manner as to leave them in no doubt that they are receiving a definite message from Him.

Being a leader amongst the saints demands great courage, especially when confronted with those who would turn aside from the word of God. Many have succumbed to the pressure due to fear filling their hearts, but it is expected that those who lead should do just this, and not become those who are led. Being valiant for the truth is not always easy, nor is it always popular, but those in responsibility cannot turn aside from it without bringing disaster into their own lives, and into the assembly where they are placed. At the same time they have to make sure that they are not standing for themselves, but for the Lord. They have to remember that they are not able of themselves to overcome, but are totally dependent upon the Lord for His aid in every situation. Humble obedience to the Lord must characterise them in all departments of their lives, for this is vital if they are to have weight with the saints whom they lead. All in the assembly must be left in no doubt that their leaders are men who not only teach the word of God, but have such a reverence for it that they shudder lest they fail to obey all it commands. The place the word of God has in their hearts and ways will no doubt be reflected in those whom they lead. Neglect of the Scriptures is the root cause of much of the departure that can be seen in assemblies, and over which many mourn. All true revivals have been marked by a return to the Scriptures, and by obedience to what was taught therein. It goes without saying, that only those who have a knowledge of what the word of God teaches, can obey it, so it follows that meditating in it day and night is essential if it is to be understood and applied to the heart. When giving instructions for future kings in Israel, Moses taught the same principle, for they were to have a copy of the law given them, and they were to read therein all the days of their lives (Deut 17:18 - 19).

JOSHUA'S COMMAND TO THE PEOPLE AND THEIR REPLY (1:10-18)

If in the previous paragraph we have God's charge to Joshua, here we have Joshua's charge to the people. What had been conveyed to him not only concerned himself, but had a bearing upon the Nation which he represented. The startling and soul stirring news was that within three days the entire people were to be over Jordan and into their inheritance. The mention of three days presents us with some difficulty, for we know that the spies who visited Rahab were three days on the trip, and may have been even a little longer before they returned with their report. It could well be that they had been sent before this announcement, and even that they had returned before it was made. The command to take with them "victuals" is interesting and reminds us of the instructions given by Moses to Israel at the Passover when they were about to pass over the Red Sea. The unleavened bread which they then carried corresponds to the victuals here. Well did both leaders know that when a multitude is hasting to pass over into a new land it has no time to prepare meals. Joshua must have had vivid memories of the night in Egypt, and the importance of having food when such difficult movements are occurring. He also foresaw that the manna would cease once the Land was entered, for it was provision for the wilderness only. Whether it had already ceased falling on the possession of the Eastern tribes we are not told, but of this we are sure, that when it ceased in Canaan, then at the latest, it must also have stopped falling there. Had the manna continued when the people settled in the Land it would have encouraged laziness amongst them, and at the same time allowed the fields, due to lack of cultivation, to become a wilderness. There is an unchanging principle in God's dealings with man, namely, that He never does for him what he can do for himself, so if food can be provided by the normal process, then He does not provide it miraculously.

There were those tribes who had no intention of passing over, for they were already settled in their portion on the east of Jordan. To them, the instructions given by Moses were re-iterated, for they were told of their indebtedness to their brethren, and commanded to pass over armed with them, so that together they might destroy the inhabitants of Canaan and obtain the inheritance promised by the Lord. These tribes - Reuben, Gad and the half tribe of Manasseh - which settled for their inheritance on the east side of Jordan, had been assisted by all Israel in obtaining their inheritance, so it was only but right that they should be told of their responsibility to repay their brethren, by engaging in the fight which lay ahead. It was no small trial for the soldiers of these tribes to leave their dear ones for several years, during which time very little or nothing about their welfare would be heard. In reading this we might think that all those numbered as warriors in these tribes were to pass over, but we learn that only forty thousand out of a possible one hundred and ten thousand actually did so. Had all crossed over, then the wives and children left would have been in danger of being overrun by the nations around them, with the result that what was already possessed would then have been lost. We must therefore view those who went over as representative of these tribes, and not every man who could have gone.

The noble answer of these Eastern tribes must have been most encouraging for Joshua to hear. They were not only willing to obey his orders, but were so zealous for him as to threaten any who would dare to disobey him. They had taken careful heed to the promises made to Joshua through Moses, and did their utmost to strengthen his courage in the vast undertaking which lay before him.

All leaders must bear in mind the importance of communicating clearly what the Lord wants His people to do. They cannot expect to be obeyed if they are ambiguous in their instructions. None in Israel was in any doubt as to what was before him, for all knew the steps they were asked to take. It will never do if in an assembly the saints are ignorant of that which is expected of them. Paul was most careful that the saints in the assemblies he planted were clearly instructed, both by his example and his word, as to how they were to function as a testimony, and as to how they were to walk as individuals. Many complain about misconduct amongst the saints, and take for granted that all know what they themselves know as to what is proper behaviour; but they may be mistaken if they have failed to teach publicly or even privately what the Lord requires of His own.

Making provision for supplies of food, especially when advances and changes are about to occur, is of great importance: a hungry people would find crossing the Jordan an exhausting experience. So too with the saints: if for example they are to engage in some special effort to spread the Gospel into a difficult area, they must be supported in their souls with wholesome food from the word of God. Doubtless the Gospel well preached has in it nourishment for the saints, but if they have not been strengthened by suitable ministry before an effort commences, they may become faint when the difficulties arise.

Just as the Eastern tribes kept their agreement to help in the possession of Canaan, so ought all saints be careful to keep their promises. Some seem to have little trouble of conscience when they fail to do what they promised to do. Often those who promise most prove most disappointing in their fulfilment. A united front with all the tribes facing the enemies in the Land was no small comfort to Joshua. It could have been taken if the Eastern tribes had not helped, but in that case there would have been a breach in the Nation which would never have been bridged. All leaders should strive to maintain unity as much as possible amongst the saints. The possession of spiritual wealth comes to all through the help of the Lord, who is pleased to use different instruments to bring it to us. It is therefore just that those already enjoying these should help others to enter into their allotted portion. We reaped the benefits of other men's labours, and it is our duty to labour for the good of those who as yet have not entered into their inheritance.

From the hearty response of the Eastern tribes to the call of Joshua we could learn that, while it is reasonable for overseers to be encouraged by a favourable reaction to all their instructions and exhortations, for they speak for the Lord and are not self-appointed men, yet in this acknowledgment of their authority, there is also a confirmation of their fitness for the work to which they have been called. Leaders must be able to lead, or else they are leaders in name only.

THE SPIES AND RAHAB (2:1-24)

A number of questions arise as we make our way through this chapter. 1) Why send spies to investigate Jericho, seeing the Lord had promised to give them success in capturing the Land? 2) Why take the risk, lest these two bring back an evil report, and so discourage the people, as did the ten spies some thirty eight years earlier? 3) Why did the two men go to a house of ill-repute and risk being ensnared by an evil woman? 4) Why did she tell lies in order to protect the spies from being killed? 5) Why did she take sides with Israel which to her was a foreign nation, and turn traitor to her own nation?

In answering the first of these questions, we are confident that the Lord was not grieved at the sending of these spies, otherwise He would have shown His displeasure at their going. In this action Joshua demonstrates the importance of using the wisdom God has given us, even when we are assured of His presence and help. For example, if a missionary is going to some new country to labour, he would be wise to make inquiries about conditions in it, and also about the difficulties he may encounter when he arrives. In doing so, he is in no way manifesting any lack of faith or confidence in God. Finding out the morale of the enemy is a very important piece of information for any invader. Waiting for the report from these men no doubt tested the patience of the people who were anxious to pass over and begin the attack. To move into a strange city and find out the information required was no small feat, and one which only those with adroitness and skill could accomplish. For men to be seen entering an harlot's house would not be unusual, so going there at the eve of darkness would not draw the attention of the inhabitants to them. Careful as they were to keep their mission concealed, nevertheless they were detected by some one who told the king of the city about their coming. We may be sure that the presence of the vast camp of Israelites on the other side of the river must have aroused the fear and apprehension of the city, and alerted them to unusual precautions lest any from it should attempt to infiltrate its defences. Possibly it was for this reason that the spies had to enter during the twilight, even at the risk of being seen, for the gates were closed after dark. There being two of them together, meant that the temptation of such a place was at a minimum. Beyond all these normal observations we have to see the sovereign hand of God in the entire mission, for if ever two men were guided by God in their movements, these were they.

The disobedience of Rahab to the orders of the king and her lies regarding the whereabouts of the spies have caused great difficulty to the minds of theologians ever since. Her deceit and disobedience have been used by some to justify lies if they be told in order to save lives. Others view her deception as evidence of her undeveloped faith, and see in it some excuse for the wrongs of young converts, who may not be aware of the seriousness of such sin in the sight of God. A third view of the problem is that in OT times we must not expect the same standard of honesty from people as we now expect from those who have the indwelling Spirit. If we think of her background and of the fact that she lived by means of her foul trade, we can be sure that such an one would have little conscience about telling lies. Indeed, in some parts of the world unless one is able to tell lies he is regarded as stupid. Of this we can be sure, her lies were told before she talked to the two spies, and before she had been assured of the safety of herself and her family.

On the other hand, she must have had some faith before the men entered her house and before she hid them in the flax on the roof, otherwise she would have chased them from her, or surrendered them to the king's messengers. Whatever be the explanation of her actions, the fact remains that they were used to the safety of the spies, and are another example of God overruling evil for good. On her advice the pursuers rushed toward the flooded Jordan hoping that they would overtake the spies, but, failing to do so and viewing the overflowing river as impossible to ford, they abandoned their pursuit and gave up the chase.

The spreading of flax on the flat roofs of houses was normal practice and the bundles afforded ample protection for the men who lay under them. Thus the woman whose corrupt ways had ruined the men of the city, was using her skill to deliver men, who were foreigners to her, from destruction. In this act we are shown evidence of her faith, so her works saved her. Not that she was delivered because of them, but rather they proved the faith that enabled her to do them. It would appear from the wording that the men were not only hidden in the roof but were about to sleep there, so they were not in any fear of danger. However, before they fell asleep they were disturbed by Rahab, who came up to them and made her confession. Her thoughts and feelings of heart were opened up while she poured out to them her full story. In it she revealed that throughout the Land the morale was at a low ebb. The news of the past victory over Pharaoh, and the more recent doings of the armies of Israel in slaying Sihon and Og had reached them and brought to them alarming facts which made them sink in despair. Thus before any attack was made upon their cities, they were already dispirited and ready to concede victory to the invaders. Whoever had brought the tidings

to them must have learned of the name of the Lord, for
she freely confesses that this story of triumph was not an
account of mere men's doings, but the exploits of Jehovah,
who is supreme both in heaven and in earth. It is normal
for those who have repented and turned to God to
imagine that all around them have the same spirit and
feelings, but this can be a mistake. While Rahab believed
that the entire people were melted under the threatening
judgments which were approaching, yet this was only
partially true, for while the trembling and dread were
present, yet there was no evidence of them surrendering
to God, or of their true repentance. Instead, they counted
upon the strong walls of the city and upon their defences
to repel the armies of the Living God. Had all the
inhabitants of the city been like Rahab they would all
have been spared, just as she was.

Following the assurance given her of her own safety,
her concern was for her parents and family circle. She
could not think of their destruction, and sought to have
them delivered by the spies. This was also granted,
provided they came and dwelt permanently in her house.
Because of her illicit trade she had lived apart from her
father and mother, but now the entire family was to
dwell under the same roof. In this we see that when
people are made right with God they are often made
right with one another. Her conversion was not a mere
escape from destruction, but a complete change of heart
and the beginning of a new life in the fear of God. When
later brought into the camp of Israel she became the wife
of Salmon, and entered the royal line which led to David
and ultimately to Christ, for she is one of four women,
Tamar, Ruth, Bath-sheba, and Rahab, mentioned in the
genealogy of Matt 1.

Those who have grasped the gravity of their position,
and have escaped from danger are always seeking

assurance of their safety. Rahab was no exception for she asked for a "true token". The one given to her was sure yet simple. The window which she had opened and through which she let the men down was on the outside of the wall, and would be visible to the armies of Israel at the time of the capture of the city. In it she was to place a scarlet thread. Some have thought that this thread was the same as the rope which she had used to let the men down. Their reason for so doing is the use of the word "this" in the passage, which to them must refer to the "cord" of v. 15. Others view the thread as a symbol given her by the spies, and something much lighter than that which would bear the weight of a man. The words used for "line of scarlet" here are used to describe the lips of the bride in the Song of Solomon where they are translated "thread of scarlet" (ch. 4:3); the idea of a rope would not be appropriate in such a context. Moreover, if a rope of scarlet were to be suspended from her window, this would have drawn the attention of the neighbours, but if a thread were so placed, it would only be seen by those who were looking for it. However, the important feature about it was that it marked out her house so that the invaders could identify it, and at the same time it gave her and her family an assurance of their safety.

There were two other conditions imposed upon Rahab by the spies, if their promise, which they gave her by oath, was to be fulfilled. First, she was not to utter to anyone that they had visited her, and secondly, all who sought safety were to remain inside the doors of her house. Like Noah in the Ark, and like the Israelites behind the blood-sprinkled doors, the family was to remain in the place of safety. It would seem that the threat of danger, and the way of escape, brought about a treble blessing to this Gentile family: 1) it brought to them the knowledge of Jehovah in whom they were placing their trust; 2) it delivered them from their fears; 3) it brought them together under one roof, something which, due to Rahab's illicit way of life, had not been enjoyed for some time.

Before the men departed from Rahab she manifested a concern for their safety. If their lives were lost, this would not only have been a tragedy for themselves and their people, but also would have nullified all that they had promised to her. In directing them to the mountains and telling them to remain in hiding for three days, she manifests a sagacity far beyond what was to be expected from one with her back-ground. No doubt the spies would be desirous to hasten back to report to Joshua, and he, in turn, would be anxious to learn how they fared, but nevertheless, all must wait, for it was better to be sure than sorry. When they arrived they gave him the grand report, couched in terms most assuring. They told him that the Land was melted in despair, and spoke as though it were already possessed. "Surely the Lord has given all the Land into our hands" was their bold statement.

There is so much in this chapter that is typical, one would be tempted to view it from that standpoint, but the purpose of our book is not so much to dwell on that aspect, but rather to learn from it something to help those who lead the saints. In one sense the man Joshua, apart from sending the spies, played no part in this grand story. Even in this, there is an important lesson to be learned, for a true leader must know how to delegate work to those whom he has helped to train for it. Quite often men have struggled to do everything of importance by themselves alone, and almost concluded that no one else was capable of doing any work, especially when it required skill and ability. Without doubt, Joshua could have claimed that he was the most qualified man in

Israel to spy the Land, for already he had undertaken this task, and proved himself to be competent at it. Nevertheless, he is wise enough to delegate this task to others, and thus allow them to have experience in a field hitherto unknown to them.

Another important feature of a true leader is evident in Joshua at this time, and should also be present in every overseer. It is to have sufficient discernment so as to select and encourage those who are fitted to do special service for God. The spies, even though young and not experienced in this kind of detective work, were judged by him to be sufficiently wise and competent to accomplish their mission. It is not only sad but disastrous for men to be encouraged by elders in an assembly to undertake work for which they are not fitted. There is not a hint in the passage that Joshua had any fear or dread that they would return disappointed, for while it was amazing to them to witness the sovereignty of God, and to experience His protective hand, it was no surprise to their master. The Lord Himself, the NT antitype of Joshua, also sent out His messengers in twos, and He likewise had the joy of welcoming their glowing reports.

Just as truly as Joshua heard the story of the returned spies with joy and satisfaction, so too have the elders of an assembly often listened to missionaries whom they had encouraged into the field, report of what they had experienced of God's workings with them. Actually the spies had accomplished more than they were asked to do, for they had not only surveyed the city and its people and discovered the low state of their morale, but had won a Gentile to the knowledge of the Lord. Rahab through her faith was not only saved from perishing, but was made one with the Nation she once dreaded, and became so intermingled with it as to lose her own nationality.

THE CROSSING OF JORDAN (3:1-17)

After a period of forty years, the dream of every Israelite was about to become a reality, for ever since the Nation was formed and left Egypt, the promise of entering into the Land of Canaan was uppermost in the minds of the people. There were times when the hopes of doing so were dim. On the one occasion, at Kadesh, when there appeared to be reasonable expectation that it would be so, unbelief proved costly, for thirty eight years had to be spent, and the rebels buried in the wilderness, before such a prospect could be realised. Perhaps the majority of those who did enter were born in the wilderness and knew nothing of home comforts, of fruit trees, of cultivation of the ground, or of the pleasure of settled life. They had however experienced something of ordinary life since the capture of the kingdoms of Sihon and Og, but this was mainly in the domain of shepherding flocks and herds. We can well imagine the excitement and wonder which must have filled every breast when this new venture was opened up to them. Not since the crossing of the Red-Sea had such a momentous event occurred. They were encamped some short distance from Jordan, so they had to move close to its banks, which meant descending into a steep valley. The flooded river must have appeared to them all but impossible to cross, and in their hearts they must have wondered why such an inappropriate time had been chosen for the crossing. The fords, when the river was low could have been forged, however slowly, but to go through the rushing waters when the river was in full spate was utterly impossible. Some might ask, "How did the spies cross over?" The answer is, that they being young men could easily swim the flooded river, but such a way was out of the question for the thousands of women and children in the camp of Israel, not to mention the loss of time in so doing.

We might wonder why God decided to allow Israel to pass over in the most difficult conditions, but we must remember that the nations of Canaan were expecting the invasion, and must have been anxious about it happening. However, the flooded river must have put them off their guard, for they could have reasonably concluded, that they had no danger to fear so long as the river was in flood. God, by overcoming the obstacle, must have taken them by surprise.

When something important has to be undertaken, especially when it is for the Lord, it is customary for His servants to rise up early to fulfil the task. This case is no exception, for Joshua rose early and directed the officers to go through the ranks of Israel and inform them of the course of action. The officers, already mentioned in ch. 1:10, although their title comes from a word meaning to "write", seem to play more than a scribe's role, both here and in other places where the title is used. Apparently they were not only acquainted with the census of the people, but were able to go amongst them with detailed instructions regarding the directions of their leader, Joshua. The three days mentioned here may be the same as those mentioned in ch. 1, and what has intervened may well have occurred previous to the intimation given there.

The prominence of the Ark here and at the taking of Jericho is no doubt of great significance, for it indicated to the people that the wonders which they were about to behold were the result of God's presence with them. Unlike Moses, who used his rod at the crossing of the Red-Sea, Joshua here was not permitted to perform directly any miracle, but to simply give the people the instructions given to him by the Lord. In normal occasions the Ark was carried by the sons of Korah, but on the occasions when miraculous workings were performed by it, the priests the sons of Levi bore it on their shoulders. We know that all priests were sons of Levi, but not all the sons of Levi were priests. It was to be carried, not only as a forerunner, but as a guide for the marching hosts. In order that all might see it, there was to be a distance of about half a mile separating it from the people. While journeying in the wilderness the Pillar-Cloud was the means of guidance, but apparently this aid had now been withdrawn, most likely because it was solely for the desert. The new way of directing was in keeping with the new path they were about to tread, which was one they had never trodden before. How the Lord communicated the instructions to Joshua at this time we are not told, but one thing is evident namely, that nothing he said to the people was of his own devising.

Just as the opening of the Red Sea had raised Moses in the estimation of the people, so this opening of Jordan was God putting His stamp of approval upon the new leader. Not that Joshua directly opened the river, but because he gave directions regarding it, and God honoured His servant in fulfilling His word to him at this time. In this experience they could not fail to discern a similitude between the two leaders. The fact that he perceived a miracle would take place and acted without doubting its occurrence, must have convinced the people that he was in close touch with God, and that he had received a revelation of the wonders which were about to occur. He not only knew what was in store, but also knew when it would happen. "Tomorrow the Lord will do wonders among you" are his words to the people (3:5). Seeing the Lord was about to manifest His power to them, it was becoming and needful that they should consecrate themselves. This implies that all ceremonial uncleanness had to be purged out. Just as leaven had to be removed from the houses at the time of the Passover, so at this time the holiness of God demanded that where His presence was there the people who were blessed with it must be holy.

In full view of the Nation the Ark was carried to the lip of the flooded river, then in a miraculous way the flow of waters dried up, because some miles up-stream they stood up in a great heap. Attempts have been made to account for this phenomenon by suggesting that the river was dammed by a huge landslide, or by some earthquake, news of which had been sent to Joshua. Of these things there is no mention in the passage.

Much has been written as to exactly where the feet of the priests stood. Some think that they remained at the spot where they first touched the water, others that they stood on the bank of the river's normal bed, and others that they proceeded to the centre of the river, and to the spot where the waters were at their deepest. Perhaps the latter is the correct view, even though many maintain that stones placed there would have been swept away at the return of the flood. This would depend upon their size, for if they were large enough and packed together, they could withstand the force of the waters.

Never at any other time did so many cross that historic river in so short a time. Not only did the people pass over, but their flocks and herds went with them, together with the wagons which contained the heavier parts of the Tabernacle. The sight of the Ark in the midst of the river was the comfort of every heart and the assurance that all was well with the hosts. The waters would sweep it away if they returned, so the people were as safe as was it. Although they did not sing, as was the case at the crossing of the Red Sea, yet they must have rejoiced at having set foot for the first time on the Promised Land. In the former crossing the enemy was behind them, but in this occasion the enemy was before them. There were no cities to be captured nor high walls to be scaled in the desert into which they first entered, but now great obstacles lay before them.

All who have sought for spiritual help in this chapter have seen in the Ark standing in the midst of Jordan a type of the Lord on the Cross. There He stood as our representative, and at the same time our assurance that the floods of judgment would never swamp us. Only the priests' feet felt the cold waters of Jordan, but He bore the full flood of the deep waters which went over His soul. Just as the Ark in type conquered the waters of Jordan which speaks of death, so He triumphed over that mighty foe, and destroyed him who had its power, that is the Devil. In crossing the Red Sea Israel was, as it were, dead to Egypt, in the crossing of Jordan they died to the desert. These crossings teach us in type that the Cross cuts us off from the world, and at the same time puts an end to the old man. There was a practical reason why there was to be a distance between the Ark and the people, but all can see in this a type of our Forerunner who has gone before us; there will always be a distance between what we experience and what He has experienced, for He has gone into depths which we will never enter.

This wonderful day in Israel's history has many lessons to teach those who lead the saints. Just as Joshua had undaunted faith in attempting to cross the flooded Jordan, so every leader can succeed as a leader only if he has full confidence in God. Likewise, he must make sure that all his instructions are clearly taught to those who are called upon to follow him. Many take for granted that all in the assembly know the truth of God, and because of this never think there is any need to teach it. We all have to confess that the mere knowledge of the word of God will not necessarily result in it being obeyed, but we equally know that where there is ignorance of it, there can be no expectation of it being heeded. The officers who went through all the host were responsible to make all aware of the time for crossing, and the way it would be accomplished. Furthermore, guides must be careful to give the Lord His rightful place, just as Joshua gave prominence to the Ark. All the glory went to it not to him, so all the glory must be given to the One to whom it belongs. It is delightful for leaders to view the progress of the saints as a result of their example and instructions, yet at the same time to be able to keep themselves from claiming the glory which belongs only to the Lord.

THE TWO MONUMENTS (4:1-24)

There is ever the possibility that great miracles and divine deliverances will eventually be forgotten, not of course by those involved in them, but by the succeeding generations. The memory of the deliverance from Egypt was preserved in the Nation by the Passover, and was intended to rouse the children to ask questions as to the meaning of its celebration. Likewise, the two stone monuments erected at the crossing of Jordan were object lessons for future generations. The Lord who gave Joshua instructions about them, designed and planned these stone pillars, and clearly indicated His purpose for doing so. The sight of twelve large stones stacked up in a heap at Gilgal, and another twelve raised up in the midst of

Jordan, could not but attract attention to any who passed that way. No doubt those at Gilgal would be the more likely to be noticed, but this could easily lead to investigating the story behind them, and so lead to the search for the same type of monument in the river. All are aware that stones from a river are distinct from those freshly quarried, in that the sharp edges have been removed by the action of the water. A glance at the Gilgal stones would quickly reveal that they were not in their original abode.

Long before these monuments were erected the father of the Nation, Jacob, had erected stones to commemorate the Lord's appearances to him (see Gen 28:18 and 35:14). There are practical reasons why stones should be used for such a purpose. First, they were readily available without cost or labour, and secondly, they were durable. As we will learn later in this book, when something lasting was to be recorded, it was invariably inscribed on stone. Even the Law was thus written. Again we notice that the colours in Revelation are those of stones, for these never change with the passing of time. It would appear that there were ample supplies of stones in the bed of Jordan, for there is no suggestion that a search for them had to be made. It may have been that some of these could have been used as stepping-stones when the river was low and could be forded. The absence of all references to bridges in the Scriptures is surprising to our minds, but apparently such structures were unknown to the ancients.

Great stress is laid upon the position where these stones were to be placed. It has to be admitted that there is much variation of opinion as to exactly where the first twelve erected by Joshua were situated. Indeed, some do not believe there were any built in Jordan, but claim that there was only one heap, the one at Gilgal. Those who see only one heap read the clause in v. 9 as "from the midst of Jordan", instead of,"in the midst of Jordan" as most of the versions read . Even though we read of no divine direction to Joshua to set up this second heap of stones, we may be sure he was not acting without it. As we have already noticed there is great difficulty in deciding the exact spot where the feet of the priests stood firm. If we accept the view that they proceeded to the centre of the river's bed, then the stones were erected in the deepest part of the river. The objection raised that stones set up in the bed of a river could not endure the swift flow of the current, can be answered by stating that the stones raised must have been there for centuries, and if large enough would withstand the flow indefinitely. These stones were not carried on the shoulders as were the other stones, but erected at the place where they were found, so they could have been quite large. The idea that stones in a river could not be seen and so would serve no purpose, is true only when there is a flood. Though the writer was living long after the events he records, he can testify that the stones were there "until this day".

The twelve men, first mentioned in ch 3:12, represented the twelve tribes, and each had the task of lifting and carrying a stone from the bed of Jordan to Gilgal where the first camp of the people was set up. Possibly a five miles journey was entailed, so they must have been relieved when the host rested for the night, and they were free to lay down their burdens. Most likely the Ark, which had stayed the flood and sheltered them from drowning, would halt at the chosen spot and round it the camp would be set up. The monument was sufficiently far from the river, to put beyond dispute, that it was not there by accident. Those who viewed it could immediately see that it was erected with stones from the river. Like all such objects, it was expected that it would arouse curiosity, especially amongst children. The parents were to use this introduction as an opportunity to relate the story of the wonderful crossing.

The place where the crossing was made was quite a distance from Kadesh-Barnea, from which the spies had been sent by Moses, and which lay some miles north of Gilgal. There was a strategic purpose in selecting this more southerly crossing, for it was designed to facilitate the capture of the Land. It saved the armies having to face the hilly and fortified part, which proved so difficult and disastrous when the Israelites, presumptuously and in spite of the warnings of Moses, attempted to take it (Deut 1:41 - 43). On this occasion, they were led to begin from Gilgal and create what proved to be a deep wedge driven across the Land, which literally divided it into two parts, with the result that those kings on the north were separated from the kings of the south. There was nothing haphazard in the advance of Joshua, for the Lord directed him not only in the several cities he captured, but also in his overall strategy of the campaign.

The spiritual lesson of this chapter is well known. The stones in the river illustrate the Nation under death and judgment, the stones at Gilgal illustrate the same people as raised to enjoy their inheritance. The believer can learn in these monuments his association with Christ, of whom the Ark was a type. In association with Him in His death, he learns that he is dead to sin and the flesh, and in associated with Him in resurrection, he learns that he is raised to walk in newness of life. In a word, the stones tell the same story as believers' baptism. The idea of haste is emphasised in the crossing and this is understandable, for the priests standing bearing the Ark would eventually become exhausted. Likewise, we notice that in the Acts period, all who were saved quickly obeyed the Lord in baptism. Indeed, any thought of an unbaptized believer seems to be out of the question. If these stones were expected to arouse, especially among children, enquiries as to their meaning, so too ought believers' baptism by immersion to stir the interest of all who witness it, and to them an explanation should be given as to what it signifies.

There is also in this story some teaching for those who are in responsibility, for just as the twelve men chosen to carry the stones represented the people, so in many respects the elders of an assembly represent it. While it was an honour to be chosen for this specific work, yet it was no easy task which was assigned to those selected. Their shoulders must have been sore when they reached Gilgal, a spot possibly five miles away from Jordan. It is impossible to be a leader in any assembly without carrying a heavy burden. The apostle, after describing the many hardships involved in his work, puts as it were their climax in the well-known words, "that which cometh upon me daily, the care of all the churches" (2 Cor 11:28). While he had a special burden as the apostle to the Gentiles, yet all who shoulder the care of the saints know in measure what it entails. In the case of the twelve stones set up in the river, only Joshua is mentioned as erecting them. They were doubtless heavier stones, yet none is said to help him at that time. This reminds us of the death of Christ, for He bore a burden at the Cross, and bore it all alone.

When all was completed in the bed of the river, and Joshua himself had passed over, he called to the priests who were bearing the Ark, "Come ye up out of Jordan". As soon as it reached the bank on the western side, the waters returned to their former flow. Perhaps this is the only occasion that we know of when the Ark was at the rear of the host. Normally it led the way, and when stationary, it was in the centre of the camp. There is a sharp contrast between the words of Moses when it set forward, "Rise up Lord, and let thine enemies be scattered" (Num 10:35), and the call to it here. If any attempt be made to suggest what is typified in this feature of the Ark's movements, it may be that the host of saved ones who went ahead of its figurative death and resurrection, illustrate those many OT saints who were landed in glory before Christ died and rose again.

The fact that the waters returned at this time proves that their being heaped up was not through natural causes. Had some landslide stopped their flow, then they would have remained dammed up for some time. Their coming back was no less a miracle than their stoppage, and all their movements were under the control of the Lord, symbolised in the Ark. We can have little idea of the feelings of the people when they first realised that at length they had safely arrived in the Promised Land. Little wonder that they had a special regard for Joshua on that day. They had been taught that their leader was in truth a man to be respected and feared, for he had not only taken the place of Moses, but had convinced them that he was not a whit behind him, as regards proving the power of God in their deliverance.

It was Passover time, the tenth day of the first month, so there was much to bring to mind that first great deliverance. How sad that some forty years had intervened! Some, no doubt, had crossed both the Red Sea and the Jordan, but the graves of the unbelievers had strewn the wilderness. Unlike the former deliverance there was no singing at this juncture, most likely because in this case the enemies were still to be faced, whereas on the former occasion the enemy was overthrown and drowned. Nevertheless, the opening of Jordan's swollen waters was no trifling matter, for the Lord's power there displayed was to be made known to all the peoples of the earth, and was to be a cause of reverential fear toward Him amongst the people of Israel.

In the camp at Gilgal was an army of 40,000 which was distinct from all the rest of the host, for they had their inheritance on the other side of the flooded river. They were the soldiers of the two and one half tribes. In crossing with the rest they had demonstrated that they believed God would give His people the Land, and also that the time for so doing would not be long. To be parted from all who were dear to them was no small sacrifice, nor can we doubt that they had many deep concerns about the welfare of their wives and children. They were going to fight for possessions they would never own, but at the same time they were paying the debt they owed to the Nation, for a short time earlier all the people had fought to obtain for them their inheritance. In a sense, they were pilgrims in the Land, even though they had passed through Jordan. No doubt most are critical of the tribes who settled for the eastern side of the river as their inheritance, and compare them to worldly Christians who refuse even to be baptised. While this was true of these tribes as a whole, yet little can be said against the noble band who fulfilled their duty by crossing over with their brethren at no small personal cost.

THE CIRCUMCISION AT GILGAL (5:1-9)

Were it not for the opening verse of this chapter, we would conclude that no more injudicious time for circumcising the thousands of males in Israel could have been chosen, for the camp was set up in full view of the inhabitants of the Land. Had any attack been made on the new arrivals, there would have been only a limited number of men fit to repel it, and these would have been in the older group. However, no such danger was envisaged, for the wonder of the passage opened through the flooded Jordan had caused the dread of God's power to so possess the Amorites who occupied the mountains and hills, and the Canaanites who dwelt along the sea coast, that they were powerless and too faint-hearted to dream of an assault. Apparently Joshua was aware of this paralysis of their spirits, and so had no concern for the safety of the camp. We need not be surprised at his conclusions, for if God could heap up waters and hold them until He was pleased to release them, then it was obvious He could just as easily cause their stout fortifications to melt before Him.

A more difficult question arises when we consider why the stay at Gilgal should be the occasion chosen by the Lord for the Israelites to be circumcised. Many a weary delay had been experienced during the journey in the wilderness, yet throughout these travels there was no attempt made to have this rite performed. We cannot help being amazed that Moses never attended to this matter, and that from the time the people left Egypt, no family or tribe thought of such a thing. In a sense the new generation which had been born in the wilderness was without the sign of the covenant which linked them to Abraham. We may not have been surprised if during the servitude in Egypt this operation had not been performed, but apparently throughout that period the sign of the covenant had been put upon all the sons born. Some have suggested that because the Israelites were constantly travelling in the desert, it would not have been convenient to delay the march in order to perform this operation, but they were not always on the move, for indeed they remained for long periods in the one place, as for example when they encamped at Sinai and received the Law. Again we must remember that it was to be performed when the child was eight days old, so all the infants would have to be carried by their parents anyway, whether circumcised or not, so this could not be the reason for its ceasing. Without totally satisfying all our queries, there appears to be in the passage the real reason for its suspension. The total rejection of all over twenty years old, because of their unbelief, and their destruction in the wilderness, seems to imply that their offspring were disowned by God and could not be regarded as sons of His covenant, so they were not allowed to wear the sign of it. Admittedly, most of those who thus died did have the sign, for they had been born in Egypt and were circumcised there, but they must have felt sad that their little ones, through no fault of their own, but because of the failure of their fathers', were left to bear the shame of being uncircumcised. We cannot believe that Moses himself was against it, for he encountered no small problem when he insisted that his own two boys be circumcised at the time when he stopped at the inn on his way to Egypt.

We are not told of the circumcision of those who settled for the east side of Jordan as the place of their inheritance. Only the soldiers belonging to them and who went over with the other tribes were at Gilgal, and of course were circumcised there, but whether there was sufficient contact with their families to follow suit, we have not been told. One thing is clear in the story, namely, that the wilderness is not the place to expect circumcision to be practised, and those who remain on that side of Jordan are never said to have fulfilled this responsibility.

Joshua was commanded by the Lord to instruct the

people to make stone knives and circumcise all the males which had been born in the wilderness. We must be surprised at the primitiveness of these instruments, but even in the case of the two sons of Moses the same stone knife was employed. Not that iron was not available, for even in the days of Abraham he had a knife to use in sacrificing, and in the service of the Tabernacle the offerers and the priests constantly used knives, not only to slay the victims but to cut some of them up into pieces. In all the wars before this the swords were made of iron, so there must have been some reason why on this occasion stone knives were to be used. Apparently they were specially made for this operation, and possibly never used afterwards. According to v. 3 it would appear that Joshua himself made the knives, and an addition in the LXX claims that they were buried with him at his death, but this seems unlikely.

The expression "the second time" does not mean that the rite was performed twice, but rather that this was the renewal of the rite originally performed either in Egypt, or at its origin with Abraham. Now that they were back in the Land promised to their ancestors and to themselves, a Land we are reminded here "flowing with milk and honey", it was a suitable time for the covenant relationship with God to be appreciated, and for the entire nation to become what it ought to be, a circumcised people. The establishment of a camp at Gilgal ended the reproach of Egypt, for until this time the Egyptians could claim, and most likely did, that God had not fulfilled His promise in giving them Canaan, but had taken them into the desert to destroy them.

The teaching involved in circumcision is fully developed by Paul in his epistles. The circumcision of Christ means that we are cut off from the flesh because of our relationship with Him and His death. "We are the circumcision which worship God in the spirit and have no confidence in the flesh" (Phil 3:3). It is no longer a physical operation, but a reckoning with God of our new relationship with Him. The practical out working of this is the mortification of our members which are upon earth. While the flesh will ever remain with us, yet we are to treat it as God has treated it, that is, as a thing that is dead. In no way are we to obey its lusts or to make provision for their fulfilment.

Just as the camp at Gilgal was for some time the rallying place of the Nation, from which they went forth to war and to which they ever returned as their base, so we must never forget that whatever our activity we need to return in thought to the Cross, and learn afresh our true position as crucified ones.

Those who have the care of the saints know only too well how often manifestations of the flesh can upset the assembly, and even at times mar its testimony. In the world at present fleshly sins are looked upon with indifference, but God is holy and He desires His people to be like Him in character. It is the responsibility of those who minister in the assemblies to keep often before the saints not only the death of Christ, but also their death in Him. None can view the Cross without having some estimation of the seriousness of sin. Joshua established the camp at Gilgal, and all leaders should likewise keep the saints near to the Cross.

THE PASSOVER KEPT (5:10)

Another interesting event took place at this time, for the passover, which had not been kept since the camp was at Sinai, was again sacrificed. The last time we are told of the passover being kept was in the opening of the second year after leaving Egypt (Num 9:5). It was made clear by Moses that only those circumcised could eat the passover, so seeing throughout the wilderness journeys this ordinance was neglected, it follows that no passover could have been kept in the wilderness. Any at Sinai who had not been circumcised, would have been only one year old so could not have eaten the roast lamb, but all who did eat had been circumcised in Egypt. It was likely that none of the feasts were kept in the wilderness, but were held in reserve until the Land was entered. A sad feature of Israel's history is that when departure from God characterised them, then the feasts were neglected, as we learn from 2 Kings, Ezra, and Nehemiah. Once restoration took place, then a return to the divine programme naturally ensued, and the appropriate feasts were kept. The present dispensation has also had dark days when the ordinances of baptism and the Lord's supper have been neglected. In some cases substitutes were introduced, and in others long intervals elapsed without any attempt to remember the Lord in His appointed way.

The eating of the roast lamb was no small comfort to those who were in some pain due to their circumcision operation. Perhaps the few days of interval were sufficient to allow their healing to begin, even if it were not fully complete. If the crossing of Jordan was on the 10th day of the first month, the day for setting aside the passover-lamb, it follows that the instruction to keep the passover must have coincided with the instruction regarding circumcision. In the passover the people were reminded of their deliverance from Egypt by the hand of Moses, and in circumcision they were caused to recognise their association with Abraham and God's covenant with him. They could rightfully rejoice that they were no longer slaves, nor were they Gentiles as were the nations around them. Likewise they could claim the help of the One who had defeated Pharaoh, and at the same time remember that Abraham's God was their God.

THE OLD CORN OF THE LAND (5:10-12)

At this time another feature of wilderness life disappeared, for after forty years of being fed by the daily supply of manna, this now ceased, and the people began to live by the produce of the Land. Here it is called "the old corn" in the AV, but some doubt this rendering and think it was the new season's crop which was then ripe that they ate. Whether or not the Canaanites left their granaries with corn in them when they fled to the defenced cities, we do not know, but the parched corn referred to here must be the stalks of the new season's crop. Changing diet is by no means an easy experience. The Israelites in the wilderness remembered the food of Egypt, and found difficulty in adopting to wilderness fare, so it must have been almost equally difficult for those who had eaten manna all their lives to become appreciative of leavened bread. It would certainly not have had the sweet and oily taste of the manna. Even to this day some food which is appetising to certain people is just as distasteful to others. Another feature of the corn bread is that it entailed labour to make it, and later on when established in the Land there would be toil in cultivating the fields in which it would grow, so all this was different from the daily delivery of the bread from heaven. One great lesson can be learned from this point, namely, that God does not provide miraculously what can be obtained in the normal way. The manna was not given to make the people lazy, but because it was needed. However, when normal food was available, then all of this angels' food ceased to fall.

Often the food of the Israelites has been viewed in the following threefold way: the roast lamb in Egypt typified Christ in His death; the manna in the wilderness, His humanity and lowliness; and the old corn in Canaan, His resurrection. Speaking of this food in the spiritual sense, we can learn that only those who have experimentally entered into their inheritance in Christ can feed upon Him as the risen One. There was never any complaining about the roast lamb, but in the wilderness the people spoke disparagingly of the manna, and so it is still; there is something humiliating and unappealing to the flesh when the soul seeks to appreciate the reproach and lowliness of Christ. All the food provided for Israel, whether in Egypt, or the wilderness, or in the Land was intended to strengthen them as well as sustain them. A hungry people would be in a poor condition for facing the enemy, or even for travelling in the wilderness.

There cannot be too much stress put upon the importance of the food of the saints. It is the duty of the elders to see to it that all in the assembly are sustained with suitable diet. God is faithful and will provide the needed food for His people, but wisdom and grace are necessary in distributing the proper diet suited for different occasions. Certainly Christ should be ministered, but in such a way as the times and conditions demand. The saints need to learn that they are associated with Him in His death and His rejection, as well as in His exaltation. There is ever the danger of them becoming partial to one aspect of His person and work, so that if another view of Him is presented, and the practical implications of it brought to bear on their consciences, they have no appetite for, or appreciation of it.

CONQUERING THE LAND
(ch. 5:13-ch. 12:24)

THE CAPTAIN OF THE LORD'S HOST (5:13-6:5)

One more important event is recorded before the attempt to fight the enemy and capture the Land is undertaken. The revelation of the Lord to Joshua as captain of the hosts of the Lord was most apposite at this time. Just as Moses had his hands strengthened by the Lord in the burning bush before he ventured to confront the might of Egypt personified in Pharaoh, so Joshua here was given this wonderful interview with the Lord at the time when he was about to attempt the overthrow of the walled cities defended by giants. It is important to note the different revelations of the Lord given to men, and to see that He was revealed to them in a manner which suited their particular circumstances. The God of glory appeared to Abraham, and this enabled him to leave Ur; the bush experience demonstrated to Moses that Israel, though in the iron furnace, was not consumed; the attendance of the seraphim on the Lord on His throne, and their cry of "Holy" seen by Isaiah, demonstrated to him how he was to prophesy to a people who had lost the sense of God's holiness.

It would appear that Joshua was taking a walk somewhere near the city of Jericho, possibly to have a look at its fortifications and to see for himself the difficulties which its capture would entail. Unexpectedly, and to his surprise, a man with a drawn sword appeared before him. Somewhat terrified by the sight, yet courageous enough to venture near to this strange warrior, Joshua cries out to him, "Art thou for us, or for our adversaries?" He seems to realise the might of this person, and to be aware that even though he was alone, yet the issues would be settled by him, so his help and not his opposition would be most desirable, if not vital. The reply of "Nay" indicated to Joshua that he was neither a soldier in the Israelite camp, nor was he fighting in the armies of Canaan. The revelation that he was captain of the Lord of hosts settled the matter, and caused Joshua to fall upon his face in deep devotion and reverent awe. He had discovered that he was in the presence of the Lord, and that he had been favoured to have this personal interview with the One whom he had often heard speaking to him. Most are satisfied that this person appearing to Joshua was none other than Christ before His incarnation, and although such appearances are called "theophanies", they might better be called "Christophanies", but no such word has yet been coined. Well might Joshua ask, "What saith my Lord unto his servant?" He desired a message as well as a vision. The reply which he received instructed him to unloosen and remove his shoes, and by so doing show his regard for the holiness of the place where he stood. The words he heard must have reminded him of his master's experience at the bush, and at the same time caused him to grasp the fact that he was not going to fight the battles of Canaan in his own strength. The removal of the shoes signified that they were defiled by the dust of the ground and therefore not suitable for the presence of God. Even in the Tabernacle and in the Temple the priests served in their bare feet.

Attention ought to be paid to the sword by the side of the Captain. It signified that what was about to befall the cities of Canaan was nothing less than God's sword of judgment. Like the cities of the Plain they had become ripe for destruction. Not only had they increased in population, but in wickedness as well. Their cup was now full, and the patience of God had come to an end. An understanding of this silences all the criticism of the Israelites invading a people, and stealing from them their treasured inheritance. The sword of the Lord was involved, so this exempted them from all blame.

These appearances of the Lord, while previews of His incarnation, are not to be confused with it. In them He took on bodily form, but when the appearances were over He returned to His former spirit form. His incarnation was entirely different, for when He became flesh and dwelt among us He assumed human nature, not for a brief period, but for ever after. Before incarnation He had only one nature which was Divine, but when He became man He had two distinct natures in one person. Throughout everlasting days He will remain in this condition.

Leading saints is no light work, and requires more than natural determination and strength to do it properly. A personal knowledge of God is vital if it is to be done for His glory. We know that there are no special revelations of the Lord given in this age, but we equally know that there are special times when He draws near to His servants and causes them to apprehend His power and holiness. Human resolve is not enough to enable any man to bear the onerous task of shepherding the flock of God. Some might have the ambition to assume such a responsibility, but even if they do attempt it, they soon learn that it is not the position they had dreamt it to be, and that they are not able to carry the burden it entails.

Although the chapter division here seems to break the narrative, yet most are agreed that the words to Joshua given in vv. 2 - 5 were spoken by the Captain of the hosts of the Lord at this time. This has caused v.1 to be put in brackets in the RV. It is really inserted here to show us the condition of Jericho when seen by Joshua and visited by the Captain. A state of siege existed even before the Israelites made any attempt to capture it. The only hope the inhabitants had was that its stout walls would withstand any bombardment likely to be hurled against them. For any of them to venture out would be playing with death, and for the gates to be opened for anyone entering might be equally dangerous, for the dreaded invaders might take advantage of this and also press inside.

The Lord's words to Joshua were not only giving him instructions as to how Jericho would be taken, but were also most assuring. There would be no doubt about the outcome, for all its mighty men and their king would fall into his hand. Never before nor since did ever any leader hear such strange directions for taking a city. If ever faith was tested in the experience of any warriors, it was on this occasion. While marching around the walls they were exposing themselves not only to danger but also to ridicule. Doing this for six days gave the impression to the inhabitants of the city that nothing serious was going to happen, and that all the army had in mind was to reconnoitre its fortifications. As in the crossing of Jordan, the priests, bearing the Ark on their shoulders, were to go before the host and march around the city every day for six days; while doing so, seven priests were to blow with trumpets. Then on the seventh day, they were to compass the city seven times, and at the sound of the long blast of the trumpets, assisted by the loud shouts of the army, the walls would fall down flat.

These instructions to Joshua bring to an end all the preparations needful for the ensuing attack on Canaan. How unlike the normal procedure of an invading army they were, but they do show that a right condition before God is more important for victory than the best accoutrements of war. The soldiers in Israel may have imagined that much precious time was being wasted at Gilgal, and that they had missed the advantage of a surprise attack, but time proved such reasoning to be entirely wrong. The apostles were in a similar position in Acts ch. 1, for they too had to wait until the Spirit was given before they could launch forth with the news of the risen Christ. "They that wait upon the Lord shall renew their strength", but alas, we often run when we should be sitting still.

THE CAPTURE OF JERICHO (6:6-27)

In spite of the apparent illogical method of taking Jericho outlined to Joshua, he encountered no opposition from the people when he told them of it. Their ready response manifested their confidence in him, so whatever he commanded, they, without question, obeyed. In this we see the traits of a true leader. He is one who not only goes before the people but has their respect, even to the extent that they undertake what to human reasoning seems to be ridiculous. He simply called, and both priests and people immediately responded. Had he been acting on his own plans, he could not have expected such readiness, but coming from the presence of the Lord, who had given him clear instructions, he could count upon His help in influencing the people. Sometimes we forget that the hearts of all men are in His hand, but we have to learn that we are indebted to Him to make the hearts of His people willing to play their part in accomplishing the various responsibilities involved in all projects undertaken for His glory.

The taking of Jericho has another important lesson for all to learn. The Captain of the Lord of hosts could easily have overthrown the massive walls by His own strength and hand. The sword by His side could just as readily have slain the entire populous and left nothing that breathed, but this is not God's way. He is ever pleased to associate His people with Himself in His doings. In the Gospel all know that the salvation is of the Lord, yet He is pleased to allow His servants the privilege of preaching the message, and of sharing in the labour involved in reaching the lost. Alas, some have concluded that seeing it is God who saves, why should any effort be made by mortal man in the matter. The Spirit was given in an exceptional way at Pentecost, yet Peter was the instrument, no doubt empowered by Him, to reach the thousands saved at that time. The grace which saves is the grace which enables God's servants to win the lost, and in the end all the glory goes to Him.

We might well ask, "Why had the Ark and the army to go round the city for six days without any result?" or "Why did not the walls fall when first encompassed?" We must remember that God is slow to anger and extremely patient with the wicked. Even after Noah was shut into the Ark, God waited seven days before sending the deluge. Had the people of Jericho surrendered on the first day, things would have been different. Not that they had any thought of so doing, but they could never claim that they were given no opportunity to repent. On the other hand, the six days trudging round the walls were a severe test to the Israelites. The entire exercise seemed to be so useless, so needless, and so time consuming, that we marvel at their dauntlessness. The sight of the massive walls must have been terrifying, and viewing such a dull and unvarying structure for so long, must have added to the monotony. We can scarcely imagine the relief which came to the host when the loud blast of the horns sounded on the seventh day, and the great shout arose which demolished the walls.

For six days the Ark was not only leading the procession, but was the centre of interest. All the noise was around it. If any ventured to peep through the windows of the houses upon the wall, their attention must have been drawn to the strange covered object which was being carried shoulder high by the priests. Though it may have appeared to them as of slight importance, yet it was in the eyes of the Israelites the symbol of God's presence, and the Ark of His strength. How fitting on this occasion are the words used by Moses at the first movement of the camp led by the Ark, "Rise up, Lord, and let thine enemies be scattered" (Num 10:35). The trumpets may have been made from rams horns, or more likely, made of metal in the shape of the horns of a ram. This was in contrast to the straight horns, or silver trumpets, which were used to call the assembly. Most, when reading this account of the marching round the city, can see in it an illustration of the work of the Gospel. Just as all the noise was around the Ark, so the Gospel message centres in Christ and draws attention to Him. Just as the sound of the trumpets appeared to be a useless exercise, so many view the simple preaching of the Gospel as of small importance. However, time proved that the means employed to capture Jericho owed its sufficiency to the power of God which accompanied it so likewise the Gospel is also effectual to the reaching of the lost, when it, too, is accompanied with the power of God.

The time spent walking round Jericho not only showed the patience of God, but manifested the faith of His people. "By faith the walls of Jericho fell down" are the words of Paul in Heb 11:30. It took more than the strong personality of Joshua to persuade the thousands of Israel to encompass the city for a whole week. Not until the final moment was there the slightest sign that what they were doing was being effective. Not a stone moved until all moved, not a gap in the walls, until they fell flat. The grandeur of faith is, that those who are exercised by it act as God directs and leave the results with Him. The marchers may have rightly conceived in their minds that they were being mocked by the besieged onlookers, for there is often reproach to be borne in the path of obedience. But the seventh day ended all this and proved that God is no disappointment; nor does hope placed in Him make ashamed. A short time before this the same people had watched the Ark go before them and open up the river Jordan. The memory of this being fresh in their minds must have strengthened their hearts on this occasion. Neither water nor walls were formidable obstacles when the Ark confronted them, for the Lord whom it represented could as easily heap up the former as He could scatter the latter.

The collapse of the walls of Jericho, however explained, meant that the Israelites could walk unhindered into the city. They had not to look for some breaches in them, for all were able, after they had raised the loud shout, to enter just were they were marching. We must not fail to notice that the day this entrance was made was one of the most strenuous for the marchers. From early morning they had gone round the city no less than seven times, which meant that they must have trudged some fourteen to twenty miles before they undertook the task of slaying its inhabitants and setting the place on fire. Possibly the excitement spurred them on, but even allowing for this the capture of Jericho must have left the army of Israel exceedingly weary. God's power is often experienced when human strength is exhausted. Some have thought that the walls sank into the ground so all could pass over the top of them, but possibly all that happened was that they were so scattered that passing over the mounds proved to be no problem. Doubtless the inhabitants would have been panic stricken, and so utterly helpless as to make unthinkable any attempt of resistance by them. There were no prisoners taken, no infant spared, for all had to be slain, even all that breathed. This was judgment without mercy, and the solemn consequence of long developed corruption. The cup of iniquity of the Amorite had at length become full (see Gen 15:16), so just as the world in Noah's day and the cities of Sodom and Gomorrah in Abraham's day were totally destroyed, so the cities of Canaan had reached the end of God's patience, and were therefore ripe for abnormal judgment.

The Lord had given specific instructions regarding the spoil of Jericho. This being the first seizure of the treasures of the Land, it was right that it all should go exclusively to Him. Like the first-fruits of the Land afterwards, it was claimed as His portion. The slaughter of all the animals and the burning of all combustible material left nothing but the metals, and these were to be given to the treasury of the Lord and set apart for Him. The storage in the Tabernacle of these spoils of battle was the beginning of a practice continued in the Temple, for it, too, was a treasure house of the spoils of Israel's enemies. It is remarkable that no such restrictions were placed upon the spoils seized which belonged to the kings on the eastern side of Jordan. Apparently only the Land proper, that is the western side, was considered by the Lord as the real inheritance of His people, and as the place from which His portion should be taken.

THE RESCUE OF RAHAB AND HER FAMILY (6:22-25)

The two spies were directed to go to the house of Rahab and bring her, and all who were gathered with her, to the place of safety. The part where her house stood was the only portion of the wall left in tact. When all was demolished around her little home, it was secure, and this was in fulfilment of the promise given her by the Lord's messengers. The coming of Joshua with his host, like the coming of the Lord to His own, was no terror to her, but rather was it the time of her deliverance. God can be selective in His judgments, for in Egypt He preserved the Israelites from the plagues which smote the Egyptians. One of the distressing facts about even modern warfare is that often the innocent suffer along with those who were the intended target, but God acts with discrimination. The two spies who had brought her the good news were the two who brought her and her household out of the city and lodged them outside the camp of Israel. However strange to her this new situation may have been, yet it was infinitely better than being in the overthrow of her city.

She reaped what she sowed, for she kept safe the spies and was herself preserved in safety from the dreadful onslaught. Uppermost in her mind must have been the wonder of her deliverance and the safety of her friends, but most likely she never thought at this juncture of what a bright future lay ahead of her. Like most at the time of conversion, the terrible danger of being lost and the escaping of hell were the chief concern of their souls. Since then they have learned, just as Rahab later learned, that God had purposes for them far beyond their wildest dreams.

FAILURE AT AI (7:1-9)

We might wonder why Joshua decided that Ai should be the next city to be captured, but the fact of the case was that it and Jericho were the two chief centres which lay between him and the heart of the Land. To have proceeded to establish the people in the fertile and richest part of the country and to bypass these two fortified places would have been the height of folly. Once they were overcome then the way was clear for advancement into the fruitful fields later inherited by the tribe of Ephraim. Had these two forts been left untouched, then the heart of their peoples may have recovered its strength, with the result that an attack could have been launched against Israel from either of them, or both of them together. Joshua was sufficiently wise and sufficiently close to the Lord to be directed so as to ensure that no such advantages remained with the enemy.

We can scarcely imagine the shock it was to Joshua and the Israelites when for the first time since he took over the leadership defeat stared him and them in the face. Until this the sun had been shining upon all that they attempted, but now the black clouds had eclipsed all their hopes, and left them bewildered and nigh to despair. The capture of Ai, after the mission of the spies who scrutinised it and reported their findings to their leader, seemed a foregone conclusion, for Joshua was advised that there was no need for all the army to attack the city, but a mere two or three thousand would be sufficient to capture it. Alas! when the assault upon it was made, the entire picture changed, for instead of its inhabitants melting before the army of Israel, the reverse was the case; the Israelites fled in disarray before the defenders. Indeed, the very language of Rahab, "Our hearts did melt" (2:11) is now the language used of Israel, "The hearts of the people melted and became as water" (7:5). Some have blamed these spies for not fully estimating the strength of the enemy, others have blamed Joshua for not engaging the entire army when making the attack, but the true fact is that even if all the forces in the camp had joined in the battle, still the result would have been the same. Unknown to them and to their leader was the secret sin which was the sole cause of the defeat. The anger of the Lord was kindled against Israel because of this, and He would no longer fight for them, nor would He allow them to escape the punishment which their sin deserved. If He was using them as His instrument of judgment upon the Canaanites, and He was, then it follows that He expected them to be obedient to His word and to respect His demands.

Doubtless the power of Ai to withstand the invaders was much less than that of Jericho, but the Lord with His people assured them of victory. Without His help, however, failure must inevitably be the result. The sorrow of having to bury thirty six bodies, and the shame of defeat, left the entire camp in deepest distress. The thought which arose in their hearts was concentrated on whether this was going to be their normal experience, or whether it was a temporary hiccup. Full well could Joshua grasp the seriousness of the situation, for if all the cities of Canaan were going to over-power his army, then there was nothing more sure than that total destruction would be the lot of him and it. It was well he humbled himself before the Lord, and cried out his sad story in His ears. The fact that he and the elders of Israel fell down before the Ark, seems to indicate that it had been brought out from its usual abode in the Tabernacle, possibly in view of the critical situation at that moment. He had not long to wait for an answer, for the Lord told him to rise up from his fallen posture, and directed him to deal with the sin which had caused the defeat. Israel had sinned in the accursed thing, which meant that the Lord could no longer be with them in their struggle. It is obvious from Joshua's prayer that he had been influenced by the example of Moses, for like his master he tells God that the defeat of the Nation would not only be a disaster for it, but would also be a dishonour to Him. If Israel were wiped out, then the only people on earth who had been chosen to spread the fame of His name would have vanished, so that not only the name of Israel would be obliterated, but the Lord's own name would suffer dishonour. Just as in the wilderness the threatened judgment had been thwarted by the intercession of Moses, so here in the Land the plea, based on the same principle, prevailed to avert the threatened disaster.

Not only was the defeat at Ai a humiliating experience for Israel, but it must have had its effect on the Canaanites, for they would take encouragement from the fact that even one of their smaller cities was strong enough to repel the invaders. This story of success would spread quickly throughout the Land, would strengthen the melted hearts, and would stiffen resistance against further attacks. Just as surely as the taking of Jericho was a stimulus to Israel and a token to them of future success, so surely was the flight of the army of Israel a token to the people of the Land of their power to defend their cities.

This sad story is not without its lessons for ourselves, and especially for those who lead the saints. The successes of the past are no guarantee that these will continue. We cannot overestimate the value of encouragement, but the Lord's help can only be experienced when we are right with Him. Often we try to excuse failure, and blame it on the difficulties we encounter, or on the sovereignty of God, or on the times in which our lot is cast. Perhaps the last thing we suspect is sin in our lives, or in the company of the saints, and that it is the cause of our failure. Not that we should always be suspicious of our brethren or sisters, and imagine all kinds of evil is secretly going on amongst them. Such a spirit is most unhealthy for our souls, and not becoming to any one who knows the Lord. Nevertheless, there are times when heart searching is needful, and when there is a real cause for exercise, so that we discover the true cause of the failure. The true leader will not accept defeat as normal, but will humble himself before the Lord, and seek to discover the cause of it. If hidden sin is present, then only the Lord can bring it to light, for His all-searching eye sees all that is done. "All things are naked and opened unto the eyes of him with whom we have to do" (Heb 4:13). Perhaps nothing tests our spiritual development like having to deal with evil. There is ever the danger of looking lightly upon it, and even trying to excuse it. But there is another danger, for we can become harsh in our dealing with it, and go beyond what is demanded by God. Our only wisdom is to view it as seen by Him, and then we can count upon His help and wisdom which can enable us to do what is right. It is ever possible to go wrong through the wrongs of others. Evils breaking out amongst the saints are bad enough, but if those who have to deal with these act wrongly in so doing, then there is a double evil.

THE SIN OF ACHAN (7:10-15)

The Lord Himself describes in detail the trespass which had taken place: 1) it was a breach of the covenant made at the time of the attack on Jericho, for it was then agreed that all the spoil of the city not destroyed by fire was to be the Lord's; 2) it was taking that which was devoted to the Lord, and so was sacrilege; 3) it was theft, for it entailed stealing from the Lord and robbing Him of His portion; 4) it was an act of deceit, for by hiding the trove the impression was given that all was as God required; 5) it was profanity, for it was a mixing of that which was sanctified with that which was common, his own stuff; 6) it was covetousness, for the items were first seen, then desired and then taken. In this detailed description of the evil committed in Israel, we learn the various aspects which a single act can have. Indeed, the sin in the Garden was in some respects akin to this one, for there also there was something taken that was forbidden; there, too, was an attempt made to hide from God; and there, too, was dishonesty, for Adam blamed Eve, and she in turn blamed the serpent. The goods taken were judged by Achan to be most valuable, even worth risking his life to obtain. The goodly garment from Shinar must have appealed to him as a rarity too precious to be burnt. The art of weaving various colours, and at times even embroidering with strands of gold was a feature of that Land. The two hundred shekels of silver would appeal to him as useful for trading, and the tongue of gold, although only a quarter of the weight of the silver, yet was possibly the largest piece of that precious metal he had ever handled.

There was no excuse for the trespass, for the Lord through Joshua made perfectly plain what was required. "Ye shall in any wise keep yourselves from the accursed thing, lest you make yourselves accursed, ... and the camp of Israel a curse" (6:18). Anyone who dared to tamper with this plain commandment was acting in defiance of God, and wilfully daring to take the consequences upon his guilty head. Had the one who stole the treasure believed he was doing what was proper, he would not have buried it in his tent floor. What has often been pointed out from this passage is the fact that though only one man was responsible for the sin, yet when the Lord was speaking of it He charges the entire Nation with it. His words "Israel hath sinned" (7:11) do not disclose who exactly in the camp was the guilty one, but levies the charge upon the whole company. This does not mean that every Israelite had sinned, but it does mean that until such time as the sin is judged, its consequence was upon the people as a whole. Some have connected this passage with "A little leaven leaveneth the whole lump" (1 Cor 5:6), but the idea there is that if sin is not judged it will spread into the lives of others. Had all in the Corinthian assembly been leavened then none was left in it who was fit to deal with the sin.

THE EXPOSURE OF ACHAN (7:16-23)

The task facing Joshua was to find the culprit who was responsible for the sad condition in Israel. The entire camp was assembled in the morning and lots were apparently taken. The guilty person was first seen to belong to the tribe of Judah; then the family of the Zarites was taken; then in the next lot the household of Zabdi was taken; and finally the man Achan was singled out as the one who was sought. It must ever be a cause for amazement that he stood until the last moment without seemingly showing the least alarm until he was singled out and charged. As he saw the net closing in upon him, he must have sensed that the Lord was directing the lot to him, yet not until confronted by Joshua and put almost upon his oath did he own up to his crime. His confession was frank and honest. He told why he took the spoil, what it was that he took, and where he had hidden it. Alas, it being in his tent involved his whole family circle for they were privy to it. Had they seen fit they could have gone to Joshua and told what was done. This would have saved the camp all the turmoil of that fateful morning. In some measure we can imagine why Achan succumbed to his covetous desires, for he may have reasoned that if he took the garment he was only taking what was about to be burned, and if he took the gold and silver he was only taking a small amount compared with the large quantity which had been salvaged. Men always find some excuse for their unrighteous acts, and in some cases treat dishonesty as though it were a sign of mental weakness.

The text, "Be sure your sin will find you out" (Num 32:23) is exemplified in this case. What will keep us from responding to the desires of our own fallen nature, is a question which we find answered in the NT, for if we "walk in the Spirit, we shall not fulfil the lusts of the flesh" (Gal 5:16). We can be sure that thoughts of the Lord were far from Achan when he was stealing the treasure. Perhaps we are not as conscious as we ought to be regarding giving the Lord His portion. Jericho was the firstfruits of the Land, and was rightfully required by the Lord for Himself. In our day He still has His rights, and expects us to give Him the first place in our lives. We owe our all to Him, and we learn that He is no one's debtor, for the Israelites who gave Him the spoil of Jericho, were enabled by Him to obtain treasures in the Land far beyond their expectations - houses they never built, orchards they never planted and wealth they never accumulated fell to their lot. Had Achan realised this, he never would have attempted to put his hand to the accursed thing.

Throughout this sad story the behaviour of Joshua is an object lesson for all who lead the people of God. His contrition, his plea, and his rent garments speak loudly to every ear as to the right attitude to adopt when sin enters the assembly. Likewise we must not fail to see that he was as much dependent upon the Lord to help in finding the offender, as he was when he was engaged in great exploits. There are times when sin is so well covered that the most careful scrutiny of man cannot discover it. In such cases the oversight can turn to the Lord who knoweth all things, and ask him to help in the finding of the guilty person. We do not resort to lots, but nonetheless, we do believe that where there is true humiliation and earnest seeking of the Lord's help, He can still bring to light the hidden things of darkness. It must be noted that Joshua did not act on mere suspicion, for not only did the lot point to Achan, but his own mouth testified of his guilt. In executing judgment in an assembly there must be clear evidence, either by witnesses or by the confession of the guilty person.

THE PUNISHMENT OF ACHAN (7:24-26)

The scene in the valley of Achor is one of the most solemn in this book. The entire family of Achan was taken out, together with the stolen goods, and all that breathed stoned to death. Over their dead bodies was raised a heap of stones, which no doubt remained as a monument to teach all the people the seriousness of sin, especially when the portion of the Lord is involved. We might well ask, "Why was such severity needful?" The punishment had to fit the crime, for thirty six soldiers died because of Achan's sin, so he deserved to die for this; as regards his family, as we have already mentioned, it was because they were associated with him in his action that they had to share his fate. It is intensely solemn to think that one of those who marched in the congregation of the Lord around the walls of Jericho, and one who shouted when the walls fell, should have such a drastic end. The great heap of stones which marked his grave were a sharp contrast to the tumbled walls of the city

THE CAPTURE OF AI (8:1-29)

After the painfulness of defeat it is not easy for any to regain the lost courage and make a fresh attempt when all had previously failed. The Lord, who was fully aware of the fear and discouragement in the heart of Joshua, once again came to his relief with the promise that He would deliver Ai into his hand.

The triumph at Jericho was going to be repeated, but with this difference: the spoils of Ai were for the people, and not for the Lord. The words of the Lord to his servant at this time were in sharp contrast to those of ch. 7:11, when He said "Israel hath sinned". Now the black cloud has cleared away and the sun once more is beginning to shine. If the Lord had demanded the firstfruits of the spoil, the people were now beginning to reap the harvest that was sure to follow. Had Achan believed this, he would not have needed to enrich himself with the spoils of Jericho. The entire valuables of Ai were the first real treasures of the Land possessed by the Israelites. These demonstrated to them that the Lord was not unreasonable in demanding the spoils of Jericho, for all the other goods captured by them would be their portion to enjoy. He is no man's debtor and will honour all who give to Him, pouring into their lap more than they ever expected to possess. Throughout this entire book there is not a hint of scarcity, either of food or drink.

The taking of Ai, though assured by the Lord and directed by Him, was not going to be the simple and easy matter which it appeared to be when the first attempt was made. On this second occasion the entire army of Israel was employed, and not the mere three thousand men were felt needful at the earlier attack. Furthermore, the method involved craft and strategy. It was the Lord's plan to use an ambush, so Joshua chose five thousand men and sent them in the dark of night to hide themselves some distance from the back of the city. The frontal attack was made by the remaining army led by Joshua himself accompanied by the elders of Israel. When the day awoke the battle began, for the men of Ai went forth to engage the Israelites as they had done previously. The plan was most deceiving to them, for the Israelites feigned defeat by fleeing before the defenders. While doing so, the men in ambush, responding to the signal of Joshua's raised spear, came by the rear and entered the city which had been vacated by the troops. Without encountering resistance, it was easy for them to set the place on fire. The rising smoke aroused the pursuing army to the fact that something serious had occurred since they left the city, so instead of overtaking the Israelites they were in confusion, not knowing whether to return or to continue the pursuit. In this state of panic, they became an easy prey for Joshua's men to destroy. Some twelve thousand men and women of Ai were slain in one day. The upheld spear of Joshua, like the upheld hands of Moses in an earlier battle, assured his army of victory; nor did he let it down until all were slain and the king of Ai taken prisoner. The unusual step of hanging the king was taken, most likely because he was regarded as the head of all that corrupt and cursed society; so he was made a curse by being hanged on a tree. Whether this hanging was before his death and the cause of it, or whether, as was usual, he was hanged up after being slain, we are not told. His body was placed at the gate of his city and buried under a great heap of stones. Like the other monument raised over the body of Achan, this one would be a constant reminder to the Nation that they had been victorious, with the Lords's help, in defeating the enemy who had once chased them, and slew thirty six of their troops.

This story presents us with a number of difficulties especially regarding the actions of Joshua at this time. We might ask is it right that such tactics as were used on this occasion should be employed by God's servant? Should any feign defeat in order to make others blunder and entertain vain imaginations? Should those engaged in the work of God in this day use deceitful means in order to win the hearts of men? Whatever be our judgment regarding the actions at this battle, one thing is sure, Joshua was not to blame for them, for he was instructed by the Lord to do as he did. The entire plot was laid, and its success assured, before one of his soldiers had taken a step in the action. What should concern us is why the Lord gave such directions at this time. Most likely He had a double reason for so doing. First, He would teach His people that, though their sin had been forgiven, yet they must know that it left consequences behind it. The strengthened and encouraged enemy was a more difficult foe to conquer, and therefore exceptional means had to be employed in doing it. Had the Lord been with the few thousands who made the first attack upon Ai, it doubtless would have fallen, and that without engaging the help of the entire army. It is painfully true that where there has been failure in the testimony the work of God is made more difficult, and efforts to reach the lost through the Gospel are more hampered. Quite a few have used this passage to justify attractions such as picture shows, musical instruments and choirs as lawful means for gathering worldlings under the sound of the Gospel, but even we do fill halls with crowds of sinners, if the power of God is lacking they will be nothing the better by their attendance. Like the "loaves and fishes" which drew the crowds after Christ, attractions which cater for the flesh cannot have spiritual value, so those who are brought to meetings by that which the natural heart of man enjoys are merely encouraged to find their satisfaction in these things. The second reason why the Lord directed this form of strategy was no doubt to prove to the people of Ai that their pride of success in the past attack, when they chased the Israelites, was the trap into which they fell to their own destruction. Quite often God allows His enemies to gloat over their success, and then when they are inflated with pride manifests His power in their destruction. The crucifixion of Christ is the standard example of this principle, for while His enemies thought they had triumphed when they saw Him dead on the tree, the resurrection manifested the true victor.

If leaders of the saints reflect on this episode in the life of Joshua, they will be made to see the importance of giving the Lord His portion, and to be deeply concerned about any attempt to withhold it from Him. At times, as in the case of Achan, it may have been done secretly, so it is only after the consequences of it occur that it is discovered, nevertheless, when there is defeat, this area of failure should readily come to mind as the one to be seriously considered. When we speak of the Lord's portion, we in this dispensation are not merely thinking of giving Him of our material things, but included in a special way in our thoughts is that devotion of heart and out-flow of praise which He rightfully expects from us. Another lesson this passage would teach is that when failure has occurred, this must not lead to despair. Sin, though very grievous, can be dealt with successfully, and God's pardon and help can be obtained. Even though its consequences are grievous, yet victory can again be achieved. Another principle worthy of attention appearing in this story is that God does not repeat His ways of defeating the enemy. He had one method at Jericho and another at Ai. Throughout the rest of this book neither of the forms of attack were adopted in the taking of cities, or in confronting the enemy. Because something has been a success in the past does not certify that it will ever be successful. Lastly, Joshua's actions at this time show that the true leader is not afraid to try again. His confidence in God and his clear guidance as to how to act were all that were necessary for him to undertake the attack. Failures and defeat are not the last word, but only a challenge to clear away the obstacles and put God to the test.

THE ALTAR AT MOUNT EBAL (8:30-35)

Joshua, having overcome the two centres of opposition, Jericho, and Ai, had opened the way for the camp to move into the fertile centre of the Land. The whole congregation, therefore, had opportunity to leave Gilgal and travel some twenty miles inland beyond Ai to the foot of Mount Ebal and Mount Gerizim. The valley which stretched before them was later the inheritance of the tribe of Ephraim. On reaching it they saw, likely for the first time, something which proved to them that the Land was indeed a Land flowing with milk and honey. All travellers in Canaan are agreed that this area is the garden of it, and that there the soil is the best which they have seen. Moses had given instructions that an altar was to be erected as soon as possible after they had entered the Land, and that on it the Law was to be written. No doubt Joshua considered that the time was opportune to obey this injunction, so he proceeded to build as directed. It has caused much amazement amongst commentators that such a religious exercise should have intervened in the midst of the conflicts involved in overrunning the Land. To them it seems incredible that the hosts of Israel should be exposed to the risk of attack from the enemies, when only a small portion of their fortresses had been destroyed. However, this was not a case of foolhardiness, but rather one resulting from acting in obedience to God and leaving the consequences with Him. Like the circumcising at Gilgal, the people were taught that in executing the will of God they need have no fears, for His presence and blessing would be their protection.

We must note what material was to be used for this altar and where it was to be built. Only whole stones were to be gathered and assembled to make the basis of it. No human artifice was to be employed, but stones in their natural state. Over these was a plaster, possibly of lime and gypsum, and upon the plaster was inscribed a duplicate of the Law. Most likely only the ten commandments were here written, and preserved in the midst of the country as a memorial of the importance of all God's words, and a reminder to the people of their obligation to obey Him.

If at Gilgal the covenant of Abraham was restored, so here the covenant of Mount Sinai was duplicated. Just as when it was first received it was written on stones, so here again it was written on plastered stones. This is the first structure build in the Land by Joshua. It will be recalled that the father of the Nation built his first altar in this very vicinity (Gen 12:6,7), and later built an altar on Mount Moriah. These, like this one, must have been built of stones, and on that latter occasion his obedience to God's word was specially manifest. There is possibly some significance in the place where this altar was erected. We might have expected that the site would have been at the base of Gerizim, where the blessings were pronounced, but no, it was on mount Ebal, the place where the curses were proclaimed. Would this not remind us of the Cross and of the one who was made a curse for us? Upon this altar were offered both burnt and peace offerings. In the former the people found acceptance before God, in the latter they shared fellowship with Him. There is no mention of the Tabernacle or of the brazen altar in the passage, but the Ark was present. If, as was normal, the Ark faced the east, then Ebal was on its left and Gerizim was on its right hand side. The north and the left remind us of judgment; even in the temple yet to be erected during the Millennium, the place of slaughter and preparing of the sacrifices will be on the north of it (Ezek 40:35-39).

Although the details of the curses and blessings given in Deuteronomy are not repeated here, yet it is clear that these were read out so that all the congregation would be made aware of the seriousness of disobedience to God, and of the blessings which obedience brings in its train. Even the little ones were present on this occasion, so that their young minds might be impressed with the importance of God's word. Some may imagine that it would be impossible for any human voice to carry so far as to be heard on two mountains facing each other, but travellers in this region have proved that this would be no difficulty, for the acoustics are such that with ease one can cry from one side to the other and be distinctly heard. God wanted His word not only to be written, but also to be spoken, so that the people might have impressed upon them at the very commencement of their entrance into their inheritance, that obedience to Him was the secret of their possessing it, and that to depart from His word would bring upon them His curse, and scatter them from it. Alas! their after history proved that this latter principle was indeed true.

It is all but impossible to over stress the importance of obedience to the word of God. Whether we look at individuals or at assemblies, the solemn fact has to be admitted that all departure from the teaching of Scripture leads to disaster. Every true leader, like Joshua, will see to it that the word of the Lord will have a prominent place in the gatherings of the saints. Whatever be the object of our assembling, there should be room for God's word in it, for it is not likely that He will manifest His presence where His word is set aside. There is something wrong with the leadership when the saints gather for several weeks, and not once is the Bible opened. Some companies have even reached the stage when they imagine that reading the Scriptures in certain meetings would be out of place. Where departure has occurred a return to the word of God has ever been the remedy, as can be seen in the books of Kings and Chronicles.

Closely linked with this establishing of the Law in the hearts of the people was the erection of the altar. The work of Christ, typified in the offerings, must likewise hold a prominent place in our gatherings. Those who lead the saints must be fully conversant with the value of that one sacrifice for sins, and know that our acceptance with God and our atonement, typified in the burnt offering, and our fellowship with God and with one another, typified in the peace offering, are the results of the work finished at the Cross.

THE STRATAGEM OF THE GIBEONITES (9:1 -27)

There are chapters in our Bibles which we could wish it had not been needful to write because they record blots in the lives of God's servants. This is one of them, for apart from it the history of Joshua would have been without a blemish. Although his mistake and error at this time cannot be excused, yet the Lord does not directly accuse him of wrong, nor judge the Nation for this blunder. The deceivers not the deceived are judged by

Him. The possibility of receiving into the congregation those who are not genuine remains with us, and the lessons this passage teaches us in that field are most valuable. In the material realm almost everything of value has been imitated, so we ought not to imagine that something unusual has happened if Christianity is professed by large numbers who are strangers to its reality.

The Gibeonites took up a distinctly different attitude toward the Israelites from their surrounding neighbours. The latter united to defend their cities and were determined to fight with Joshua, as had the inhabitants of Ai. No doubt the early success of that encounter gave them some encouragement and hope of success. The leaders of Gibeon thought differently, and decided to obtain their escape by acting wilily. In doing so they were acknowledging that they had no hope of defeating the power of God which lay behind Joshua's success; but on the other hand, they must have realised that their bluff would be detected, and that it could result in their complete destruction. Indeed, had Joshua and the elders acted as the Gibeonites themselves would have acted if they had been deceived, the outcome would have been very different, for the covenant made would have been regarded as worthless seeing it was obtained by falsehood.

Whatever differences there may have been amongst the various kings in Canaan prior to the invasion, these were disregarded at this time, that with one voice they might present the most formidable opposition to Joshua and his army. However, one of the greatest cities of the Land took its own course and refused to join in the confederacy. The tidings of the fall of Jericho and Ai had different effects upon the minds of those who heard them. Some thought of resisting, some thought of appeasing the invaders. Instead of waiting until Joshua was on their door-step, the Gibeonites decided to send an ambassador to the camp of Israel, and in so doing win at least their lives. A problem arises in v. 6 where we are told that the camp of Israel was at Gilgal. This has caused not a few to believe that the closing verses of ch. 8 are out of place and should have been inserted at the end of ch. 11. Those who think in this way believe that the Gibeonites went to the Jordan valley where the camp was originally situated. If all the congregation including women and children had travelled from this Gilgal to Mount Ebal, it is passing strange that they trudged back to the place from whence they had set out. The solution to the difficulty lies in fact that there were several places called Gilgal, one recently named by the Israelites when they crossed over Jordan, another known to Moses (Deut 11:30) long before this. The Gilgal of this chapter was most likely the one situated in the tribe of Ephraim, and not far from Shiloh. This meant that the headquarters of Israel, instead of being in the remote corner at the south east near Jordan, was now in the heart of the Land.

The Gibeonites knew that if they were recognised as inhabitants of the Land there was no hope of their escape, so their device was to pretend that they were from a different part of the world, and that they posed no threat to the new dwellers in Canaan. In their artifice they acted with great shrewdness, for they made as sure as possible that nothing would give their game away. The old wine-skins, the old clothes, the mouldy bread, and the clouts upon their feet were uttering a united voice which told out the fact that they had travelled far, and were not aware of any recent happenings such as the fall of Jericho and Ai. Their story was believed, especially after their mouldy bread had been tasted by the elders in Israel. The vital thing which they were intent on securing was a league or covenant with Joshua. They had in their minds the thought that one so noble as he would not break any solemn agreement he would make. The motive for their coming, they claimed, was the respect they had for the name of the Lord who had done such great wonders in Egypt. Had their claim been true, their confession would have been like that of the Queen of Sheba, who was moved to visit the Land because of the fame she had heard of the Lord in Solomon's day. However well they camouflaged themselves and their goods, we might feel some surprise that Joshua did not detect that there was something wrong, for one thing was clear, if they had the reverence for the Lord of which they spoke He had not provided for them as He did for Israel in the wilderness. However, their testimony was so convincing to Joshua and the elders that he made a convenant with them that they should live, and confirmed it with an oath.

In the short space of three days the deception was revealed, for the Israelites moved into their cities and discovered, to their amazement, that the people they thought were from a far country were actually part of those who were to be utterly destroyed. They could do nothing about the inhabitants of the cities of the Gibeonites, for they had sworn to spare them. While honouring the solemn oath by not slaying them, they decided that though their lives would be spared, yet their portion would be perpetual slavery. Their task would be to cut and carry the wood for the burnt offerings, and to carry water for the laver and the other washings associated with the Tabernacle. The saddest comment in this episode are the words "asked not counsel at the mouth of the Lord". Had Joshua done so all would have been different, for all things are naked and open unto His eyes.

We must feel rather surprised that no rebuke from the Lord is recorded for this blunder. He, in His wisdom and grace, overruled the mistake here made by directing Joshua and the elders in Israel to condemn the Gibeonites to perpetual slavery, not in general service for the people, but for His own dwelling. Though unworthy to live, they were a great relief to the people, in that they freed them from the heavy task of felling trees and cutting wood, most arduous work especially in a hot climate, and from the labour involved in drawing and carrying water, also a chore none wanted to be compelled to do.

The sparing of the Gibeonites seemed totally wrong in the eyes of the people of Israel, so on this solitary occasion in this book, they murmured against the princes. However, the stand taken by Joshua and the elders to uphold the oath was not changed, so the congregation had to submit to the firm decision of their leaders.

There is an apparent difficulty in reconciling the gracious attitude adopted by the spies in dealing with Rahab, and the stern measures expected to be used in dealing with the Gibeonites, had their identity been obvious. Doubtless it was God's instructions to Israel that all who breathed in Canaan should be slain. He also made clear that their hearts would be so hard that they would not surrender. However, we do not know what would have been the outcome had the Gibeonites approached Joshua openly and pleaded for mercy and for their lives to be spared. Very likely he would have sought divine guidance on the matter and acted according to God's directions. All know that true repentance is a bar to judgment, and that many of God's threats have been nullified when those threatened sought His mercy. Indeed, the fact that neither the Gibeonites nor the Israelites were judged by Him because of this whole affair might suggest that He was not greatly grieved at what had occurred.

Most will agree that many difficulties arise over the important matter of reception into assembly fellowship. Few companies can claim that they have never made a mistake in this responsibility. The handling of the Gibeonites by Joshua and the elders of Israel has much to teach us regarding this subject. If all who apply for fellowship were genuine no problems would arise, but, if mistakes are to be avoided, discernment is essential in knowing how to act when those who are false seek reception. Quite often the oversight of an assembly has been thrilled as it listened to one tell of how the Lord exercised his heart and led him to seek assembly fellowship. To receive such is a joy and a cause of thanksgiving to God.The problem arises when someone can tell an almost identical story, but is hiding the true motive of his heart. In spite of the good show put up by the Gibeonites, there was something about the whole matter which may well have aroused suspicion. The oldness of everything and the worn out clothes were very different from those of the Israelites; their clothes did not wear out, nor was their bread mouldy, for it came fresh every morning. Perhaps another feature of the unreal is the lengths to which they will go to try and prove that they are genuine. A truly genuine man never thinks he has to go out of his way to impress upon others his sincerity. Perhaps the secret of avoiding mistakes in reception is to be much before the Lord for His help and guidance in the matter. It is worthy of note that the Lord Himself spent the night in prayer before He appointed the apostles.

The most solemn aspect of reception is that if the unreal are received then they may remain, for even though they show no signs of life, yet there is no

Scriptural authority for excommunicating them. Like the Gibeonites, they have been brought in and must be allowed to stay. Of this we can be sure, no unsaved person will ever be happy in the assembly where the Lord's presence is enjoyed. To him it will be drudgery and boredom, unless, as alas is sometimes the case, some entertainment for the flesh is introduced which is altogether to his liking. If all the facts were known we might discover that the insistence of some that instrumental music, social evenings, and playing of games are essential for holding the young in assembly fellowship, springs from the need to cater for the appetites of those who have no indwelling Holy Spirit. It is impossible to make spiritual things attractive to the natural man, so we are foolish in attempting it.

Sometimes the question arises in our minds, "do the wrongs of others and their deception of us justify our ill treatment of them?" This experience of Joshua drives any such thought out of our minds, for he was careful not to allow the wrongs of the Gibeonites as an excuse for his wronging them. At a later time Saul slew the Gibeonites, perhaps thinking that in so doing he was honouring God by avenging the deceitfulness of their forefathers, but the judgment of God was the result and years of famine fell upon the Land for his action. The true leader keeps his solemn vows even though dealing with deceivers, and because of this he ought to be very careful before making any promise.

Perhaps this is the only occasion in the book of Joshua where the people are seen to differ with their leaders. The princes stood firm because they had sworn by the Lord the God of Israel. It is a clear example of the importance of leaders not being led by the congregation. Far too often the elders in an assembly, after careful consideration, come to a united decision as to how they will act in a certain situation, only to learn that the company they lead does not agree with their judgment. The temptation in such circumstances is for them to yield to the popular opinion, and in the interest of peace and harmony, change their minds. The result of such weakness is that the assembly is leading the elders, and not the elders leading the assembly.

THE BATTLE OF BETH-HORON (10:1-43)

Following the collapse of Jericho, the victory at Ai, and the capitulation of the Gibeonites, a considerable stretch of the southern part of the Land became the possession of the Israelites. It must be noted that in each of these successes the method used was distinct. There was no trumpet blowing at Ai, nor were there any swords used with the Gibeonites. Thus God was teaching His servant that there was nothing stereotyped in the warfare, and that each new venture required fresh help from the Lord to adapt to the changed tactics. Now in this new engagement with the kings of the south, again all is different, for in this case the attack was not initiated by Joshua but by the confederate kings.

The Gibeonites' action in seeking agreement with Joshua, and handing over to him their cities without a struggle, which were larger and more important than Jericho and Ai, was a cause of great anger to the king of Jerusalem. He determined to wreak vengeance on them for their fifth columnist behaviour, and for the surrender of their great cities to the insurgents without the slightest attempt at resistance. In order to strike a death blow to the quislings he enlisted the help of four other neighbouring kings. Possibly neither he nor they felt free to risk a direct conflict with Joshua, but expected to be successful with an attack on the Gibeonites. These being neighbours, meant that he would have had no difficulty in assessing their strength. The might of the army of the united kings was far beyond anything the Gibeonites could match, so unless help came they would be sure to perish. A glance at the map will show that these four kings who came to the help of Adoni-zedec reigned in the territory south or south-west of Jerusalem, so if they lost their domain, then the large southern part of the Land would be in the hands of the Israelites. In their distress the Gibeonites summoned the help of Joshua, and in so doing brought him into direct conflict with these kings. This being the first time that he had confronted the combined force of several kings, and also the first time that the initiative was taken by the enemy, we can well understand his sense of fear. However, the Lord soon dispelled this by promising his complete victory. He was assured by Him that not one of the enemy would survive, so all their possessions would become the portion of the Israelites.

The sudden attack by Joshua must have taken these kings and their army by surprise, for they fled before him and sought shelter in any of the cities they could reach. Had their escape been successful they would have remained as enemies to fight another day, but the Lord did what Joshua could not do, for He sent down a hail-storm upon the fugitives, which killed more that those slain by the sword. They learned that God has many weapons in His armoury, and can use them as required. A scattered and fleeing army running over the open country was a vulnerable target for the large stones of ice which fell thick and fast upon them. In spite of the early success, it became clear to Joshua that he could not possibly destroy all the host which had launched the attack in the course of a normal day, so he did what none before or since his day ever thought of doing: he asked the Lord to extend the daylight until his enemies were destroyed. Well he knew that the Lord who had sent the hailstones had control of the heavens and could just as easily cause the sun to rest as He could stir into action the destructive storm. His call to the sun and moon was not a secret plea, but one spoken in the sight of all the people, so they knew that the extended day was the result of their leader's request. The day was so unique that a record of it was made in the famous book of Jasher. Perhaps no event in Scripture has caused such a stir amongst scientists as has this one. In many of their minds, if the sun were to stop, or as we know it the earth were to stop in its revolutions, then the entire planet would be destroyed, for all upon it would fall off. However, they overlook the fact that the maker of the worlds could easily have made sure that this did not happen. Something akin to this miracle took place in the days of Hezekiah when the shadow on the sun-dial returned ten degrees. His light had almost been extinguished, but he was spared another fifteen years, so the sun-setting was delayed.

The five kings who had escaped the slaughter were able to find shelter in one of the many caves. When Joshua learned of their whereabouts, he ordered that a huge stone be put upon the entrance to the cave, so instead of it being their place of safety it became their prison. To spend time dealing with these kings would have hampered the warfare and allowed the possibility of many of the enemy finding shelter in the cities. Now that they were secured in the cave there was no need for haste, since they could be dealt with later. Joshua's main concern at this vital hour was the defeat of the fleeing host, for well he knew that an army on the run is more vulnerable than one surrounded by walls in a fortified city. In spite of all his success, however, some of them did manage to escape.

When the army had consumed all the enemy except those who had fled to fortified cities, Joshua commanded that the cave be opened in which the five kings had taken shelter. When he brought them out he made an exhibition of them, and commanded the captains to put their feet on their necks, and thus made them samples of the success the Lord would give Israel in defeating all their enemies. They were slain and their bodies hanged upon trees until nightfall when they were taken down and buried in the cave. Thus their place of refuge became not only their prison but eventually their tomb. A large heap of stones placed at the cave's mouth assured that none could easily remove their bodies. These stones became another monument in the Land, and a silent witness to the people of what the power of God could accomplish when working for them.

Before we proceed to deal with the rest of this chapter, we might well stop and consider some of the lessons its earlier verses have to teach us regarding true leadership. One of these that must strike every reader is the varied methods of the enemy, and the no less varied means needful to defeat him. There are times when we must take the initiative, but on other occasions we have no choice, for the attack upon us demands our action. It is our responsibility to wrest from Satan all of our inheritance in Christ that he would claim to be his; on the other hand, as Eph 6 makes clear, the enemy may attack us, so we must use our armoury in defence; even the sword there mentioned can play its role in the struggle. The temptation of the Lord in the wilderness is a clear example of Satan moving on the offensive. It would be wonderful if all his attacks were as successfully overcome as was the case here with Joshua. Indeed he turned what looked like a defensive struggle into an offensive battle. It is well to be ready to face the foe, even when he appears to have an united and powerful force arrayed against us. It is vitally important for leaders at all times to remember that the battle is not theirs but the Lord's. Another encouraging feature of this part of the story is to see how vast is the armoury at our disposal. Whether it was by the hailstones or by the arrested setting of the sun, Joshua was assured that the entire universe was at God's command. Likewise, those who have the burden of leading the saints must ever keep in mind the resources available to them. The God who hearkened to the voice of His servant still hears the cries of men, and can do wonders which they never thought could happen. It is important for those who direct the warfare to know when the enemy is being defeated. Perhaps we are more conscious of our defeats than of our victories. There are times when the Lord is working in a mighty way and thinning the ranks of the enemy, on such occasions we might give up the struggle too soon. In these days when there is so much human organisation involved in the work of God, much that could be done is left undone because of some prior arrangement. Paul was tempted to leave Corinth, but was told to remain for the battle was not over; and earlier when he was called to Europe, he was free to respond. Peter also was not fettered by arrangements when called to the house of Cornelius. On the other hand, those being led must not become weary, even if the time is extended. Admittedly, this day of conflict was the longest ever experienced by any soldier, so many in the ranks of Israel's army must have been strained to the point of exhaustion, but the success granted was no small stimulus to them in their pursuit of the enemy. Just as Joshua inspired courage in the captains of his army, so all who have a knowledge of God and of

His ways of working must try to instil into the minds of their followers something of their own spirit. Like the mound of stones at the cave's mouth, there are still monuments dotted over many lands which prove the power of God. The victory at Makkedah was never to be forgotten in Israel, so leaders should ever remind the rising generations of what God has done for them in the past.

The hanging of the five kings is a fitting picture of those enemies which have been crucified, and over which Christ has triumphed in His death. However, it is one thing to know of the victory He gained, and quite another for us to experimentally overcome. The experienced guide can confidently teach those coming after him that there is the grand possibility of mastering every opposing force. In the days which followed Joshua's death, the Nation was content to put the enemy under tribute, so to-day many think if they can curtail to some degree the activity of Satan and his agents, they have done all that is possible.

One more lesson appears in this passage which should be noted. Joshua was always alert regarding the timing of his assaults, so when he made them he was constantly taking the enemy by surprise. On occasions this entailed marching his army for a whole night. Not every leader is capable of making quick decisions, and there are times when patience is wisdom, but when an enemy has to be defeated the less time given him to mobilise his forces the better. This is specially important when he is on the run, for if ever he is given time to re-group his forces, he can put up much stronger resistance. Not a few of the older workers believed that one of the difficulties of present day efforts in the Gospel is that they are announced far too long before they commence, and because of this announcement in advance, Satan and his associates have time to organise opposition.

After the hanging of the five kings and their burial, Joshua proceeded to capture the cities that were dotted over the southern plain. The first of them to fall was Libnah which lay directly south of Makkedah. Its treatment was similar to that handed out to Jericho: all who breathed were slain, including its king. However, in this case the spoil was not burned, for it became the property of the invaders. A like fate happened to the inhabitants of the next city taken which was Lachish. It lay further south, so the advancement was concentrated on the southern part of the Land. This city evidently put up greater resistance than the previous one, for not until the second day of attack was it overcome.

The king of Gezer, who no doubt had learned of the taking of Lachish, thought he should assist the king of Lachish, so he ventured an attack on Joshua's forces, only to be wiped out, both he and his people. Thus whether it was defence or attack, the enemy was no match for Joshua and his army. The next advance was toward the west to the city of Eglon. It fell in one day, and suffered the same treatment as Lachish. Had Joshua continued westward he would have reached Gaza, but instead he turned east and attacked Hebron. This well-known place later became the portion of Caleb, but here its initial defeat and destruction is briefly mentioned. It would appear from the words "went up" that it was situated on the top of a hill or mound, and that it had satellite cities grouped around it. Again the words are repeated, "He destroyed it utterly, and all the souls that were therein".

Instead of continuing east as he had been doing, Joshua turned toward the south and attacked Debir. It was treated as the former cities, and this meant that all in it were slain. Great stress is laid upon the fact that this total slaughter of the Canaanites was not in response to any desire in the heart of Joshua for blood-shedding, but what he was doing was entirely at the command of God. It was therefore no common warfare, but rather a purging of the earth from those who had corrupted it. In other words, the armies of Israel were doing what the fires of Sodom had done in a former day. Moreover, if Joshua had consulted his feelings and stopped short of what he was commanded, he would have been punished for his disobedience.

The area now subdued is in a summary way surveyed at the close of the chapter. It comprised the Land later possessed by the tribes of Judah and Benjamin. The extremes are mentioned, such as Gaza on the west, Gibeon on the north, Kadesh-barnea in the south-east. The country of Goshen cannot be the Goshen in Egypt, but was possibly named after it. Most likely the camp here called Gilgal to which Joshua returned was not that situated on the banks of Jordan, but was also newly named after the first camping site.

Although all these cities were captured and devastated at this time, it has to be admitted they were re-taken by the Canaanites or the Philistines at a later date, and so had to be fought for again. Indeed, not until the time of David was Jerusalem firmly in the hands of Israel, and the re-taking of it was a feat of no ordinary magnitude. Vital to the cities of Canaan were their springs or water courses. In this campaign these were also secured by Joshua. How long this effort lasted we are told, but it was certainly accomplished in a remarkably short time. The Lord is not only a great worker, and a perfect worker, but He can do much in a brief period. Six days saw creation leave His hands, and even less time was needed for Him to destroy Pharaoh and his army, and only a night passed before He, in the morning, rained destruction on the

Cities of the Plain.

We sometimes sing, "Each victory will help you some other to win". Certainly these verses show that victory led to victory. Leaders need to know that encouragement in the work of God is no small mercy, and that full advantage should be taken of every advancement in the work, even though some of the saints who are involved in it may be weary. In assemblies where two or three weeks are considered the limit for a Gospel effort, the saints cannot understand how men in the past continued for months, because the Lord was working with them. Just as these cities were taken one after another, so the Gospel has reached home after home, and at times district after district. The power of the enemy, which had held sway for years, has often been broken to the amazement of both saints and sinners. While every day is not a hey day, yet we often limit God, and fail to realise that the One who has wrought mightily in the past has lost none of His power. The one thing that kept Joshua and his army advancing was their realisation that they were fulfilling the will of God. Surely we, too, can rightfully claim that whether we are spreading the Gospel, establishing testimonies for God, or strengthening existing assemblies, we are doing what He commands us to do.

It is not the will of God that Satan holds in his grasp the souls of men and women, nor is it His will that saints should be debarred from enjoying their inheritance in Christ. Have we reached the stage when we can sit back and mourn over the success of the enemy, and feel in our hearts that nothing can be done about it? Joshua never thought of saying to his soldiers, "The enemy is very secure in these cities, and while we ought to possess them, yet we are not able to do so". Each one of them was to him a fresh challenge to prove the power of God.

THE BATTLE OF MEROM (11:1-15)

In the opening verses of ch. 9 we learn that the entire Land was united in opposing the invaders, but this vast combination was upset by the refusal of Gibeon to join in it. In ch. 10 we see that Joshua drove a wide wedge between the southern and northern peoples, and did it so suddenly that the northern forces had no opportunity to join in the fight. However, this by no means weakened the determination of the northerners to oppose the armies of Israel with all their united might. Just as Adoni-zedec had mustered the armies south of Jerusalem, so Jabin king of Hazor took the lead in assembling the armies in the north and west. These combined forces were by far the greatest show of strength ever mustered against Joshua. Until this time the conflict was between the infantry of Israel and the infantry of the Canaanites, but on this occasion the enemy was equipped with horses and chariots. No doubt the contacts between Egypt and Canaan, before and during this period, account for the availability of these powerful aids. Likely since the Israelites left Egypt, they had never encountered anything so frightening on the battlefield. The prancing of war chargers and the rattling of chariots must have caused terror to rise in their hearts, for they were merely infantry men and knew nothing of such warfare. The high-walled cities, which they had previously attacked, were designed for defence purposes, whereas the chariots were specially intended for attack, and were most likely to prove effectual on the open plain. Although some of the later kings in Israel did assemble horses and chariots, it was never God's intention that His people should employ these, but rather that they put their confidence in Him.

In mustering his army, Jabin took in a vast area, so that all the kings, whether they reigned to the north, east, or west of him, mobilised their armies in support of his cause. It is most unlikely that all these nations, Amorites, Hittites, Jebusites and others, were ever on friendly terms with each other, but on this occasion all their differences were submerged and a united front was secured, with the sole aim of defeating the invaders. Possibly, never before nor after was such a vast army assembled in Canaan. Little wonder the Lord appeared to Joshua and encouraged him yet another time with the message, "Be not afraid because of them: for to-morrow about this time will I deliver them up all slain before Israel" (v. 6). If somewhat daunted at the immensity of the task which lay before him, this word from the Lord stilled his fears, for it assured him of victory, as well as giving him guidance as to how he was to treat not only the people but also the horses and chariots.

We must take into account the importance of the earlier victory won in the southern part of the Land, for had this northern host been arrayed against Joshua and a similar attack launched from the south at the same time, his position would have been indeed precarious. As it was, he had nothing to fear from behind, but only to face the foe which lay before him. The place of battle chosen by Jabin was by Merom, a small lake where the three streams which form the Jordan are said to unite. Once again the suddenness of Joshua's attack proved fatal for the enemy. The onslaught was so successful that the great army scattered in all directions and the Israelites pursued them to the utmost limit. All who failed to escape were slain and the chariots with their horses were treated as the Lord directed, namely, the chariots burnt and the horses ham-strung. The struggle was not prolonged, for the Lord had said to Joshua, "To-morrow about this time will I deliver them up all slain before Israel". While Israel is mentioned in the statement, yet the true victor was the Lord Himself. This day was to Joshua not unlike the day he had experienced some forty odd years before, when at the Red Sea, the horses and chariots of Pharaoh were about to fall upon the Israelites, and were swallowed up in the waters. As in this case, the Lord alone was the victor and proved Himself to be indeed "a man of war".

While the initial operation was completed in a brief period of time, the "mopping up" must have extended for several years. Every settlement throughout the Land was attacked. Jabin the king of Hazor was also slain, and his city, like Jericho, was burned with fire, for it was the great centre of power at that time. The lesser cites were not burnt, only the spoil was taken out of them, but all who breathed in them were slain. There was apparently a parallel between the southern campaign and this northern one. In both a chief city was burned; in both the lesser centres were rifled; and in both there was a prolonged operation mopping up the enemy.

We must wonder that the horses were not slain, but rendered useless by the treatment given them. Once a horse's ham-string was severed it would never unite again, so it would be lamed for the rest of its life. These horses would never draw another chariot, and, though spared, presented no temptation to the Israelites, which they might have had they been left unharmed. What purpose they would serve, if any, we cannot discover. Of this we are sure, that most if not all the horses of Scripture were used for war, and for no other purpose. When noble men were travelling they used either donkeys or mules, but apparently never thought of riding on horses. In Revelation 19 when the Lord appears to set up His kingdom, He will be riding on a white charger, whereas when riding into Jerusalem, as recorded in the Gospels, He was on the back of a colt.

THE DESTRUCTION OF THE GIANTS (11:16-23)

There has been little or nothing said about the giants of Canaan until this chapter. We are told that there was only one Nation of the entire population which surrendered to Joshua. All but the Gibeonites had hardened hearts and put up as much resistance as possible. The Lord is said to have hardened their hearts so that they fought to their own destruction.

In this respect they were like Pharaoh whose heart the Lord hardened, but not until he himself had hardened his own heart. We can safely conclude that before Joshua arrived the hearts of these Canaanites were already hardened in sin, so the judicial hardness, here said to be of the Lord, was but the climax of what was already there. The closing verses of this chapter show us how Joshua dealt with the giants. It will be recalled that it was the sight of these great men which terrified the ten spies, but Caleb said they would be "bread for us". Here the loaves, as it were, are eaten up, for they are taken out of their cities and slain. Apparently the attack upon them came at almost the end of the campaign. Only after the army had witnessed many victories, and so was experienced in warfare, did it encounter these formidable enemies. However we must notice that some of the chief cities, later headquarters of the Philistines, were not taken. Not until David's day were all the giants destroyed. It must be remembered that not all the Land captured at this time was re-occupied by the Israelites, for many of these strongholds had to be re-taken in later years, so while the enemy was subdued and defeated by Joshua, it was not exterminated, but many lived to fight another day. The brief statement at the end of the chapter, "The land rested from war", indicates that the conquest, as far as Joshua's responsibility for it was concerned, was now ended. To him, an octogenarian, it was no small relief to lay down the sword, and to look over the entire Land with the knowledge that no foe in it had been able to withstand his attack, neither had the Lord failed him in all the mighty task he had undertaken.

The spiritual lessons of this campaign are indeed precious. One thing is clear, that those who lead the saints have no need to fear the attacks of the enemy, not even when he rises up with a united front. If our inheritance is to be possessed then the enemy must be encountered, for he will not give up without a struggle. There are times when his forces seem to be so overwhelming that despair would steal into the hearts of even the most experienced. Who can tell the value of a word from the Lord on such occasions? Good indeed is it for an assembly which has those in it who can convey this appropriate ministry. We would wish to avoid similar crises, this is perhaps because we are slow to learn that true progress is often the result of conflict. When the enemy is quiet we may be sure that his domain is not being disturbed and that we are failing to wrest from him the spoils which are our due. When these cities were ransacked by Israel and their spoils brought into the camp, what heaps of wealth filled the tents of the conquerors! An increase of spiritual wealth is no light matter, and well worth the struggle that is involved in obtaining it.

The temptation for saints to-day is their attempting to use the enemy's methods in their warfare. Just as Joshua was directed by the Lord to destroy the horses and chariots, so the same Lord would have His people shun in His service anything used by the world to advance its aims. Great attractions are mounted in many circles to attract and excite the crowds, but the weapons of our warfare are not carnal, so we must leave the music and the bands and the solos for worldlings to employ, and count upon God to use His own word to fulfil His purpose. It would have taken some training to have fitted Peter or any of the other apostles to lead an orchestra. The Gospel trumpet sounding loudly and clearly proved sufficient in the early days not only to gather the people but to see them saved. Had some of the counsellors around to-day been with Joshua, they would have advised him to make good use of the horses and chariots, and pointed out to him how helpful they would be in attacking the enemy, and even in carrying home the spoils. The Lord saw otherwise, and still does see differently from the reasoning of carnal minds.

When the Lord ascended on high He gave gifts to men. These gifts, like the spoils captured by Joshua, enrich the people of God. It is heart stirring to witness the Lord using in His service those who were once the instruments of Satan. In the exercise of gift the wealth of the Lord is distributed amongst His people. The distributors of it have nothing in which to glory, for they are simply passing on to others what the Lord in His grace has given to them. The unsearchable riches of Christ, which Paul preached amongst the Gentiles, were treasures for the heart and soul which money could not buy. At Ephesus, where he shared out most of his store of spiritual wisdom, he had to fight with beasts. Like all who engage the enemy and spoil his goods, he knew the hardships of conflict. Many would desire to become wealthy in spiritual experience, but few want to pay the price involved.

The attack on the giants has also its lessons for both leaders and those they lead. An obvious one is, that what seemed a terrifying obstacle to possessing the Land when first viewed by the spies, turned out to be nothing alarming. Quite often the foes we most dread are much smaller when we are confronted by them than we had thought them to be. Another lesson we can learn here is that God in His wisdom does not allow us to encounter the strongest forces until we have experience in our spiritual warfare. Perhaps we could add yet another, namely, "The clouds we so much dread" seldom are as black as we expected them to be.

A REVIEW OF THE VICTORIES GAINED (12:1-24)

With the completion of this northern campaign, which must have taken about five years, the entire Land was conquered and ready to be distributed amongst the tribes. In order to leave on record the extent of the warfare and its success, this chapter is devoted to a grand summary of the different wars waged and the many kings destroyed. In the survey, the area captured involved the territory taken before Jordan was crossed, as well as those parts taken by Joshua in the western side of the river. In the earlier record of these later victories only a few kings which had formed a league to make war with Israel are mentioned as having been slain by Joshua. In order to give a full picture of the vastness of the conquest, a complete list of all the kings slain is given. This covers from the defeat of Sihon and Og in the days of Moses, until the northern confederacy was conquered as recorded in ch. 11. The success story proclaims loudly and clearly the omnipotence of God with His people. No doubt the first great victories on the other side of Jordan were samples of what was in store when the Nation passed over into the Land proper. They are later renowned as outstanding examples of divine power, not only in the camp of Israel, but also in the minds of the Canaanites. This territory was not only captured, but was distributed by Moses to the two and half tribes which chose their portion in that area. Much has been written and preached about their failure to pass over Jordan and have their possessions amongst their brethren. However, no complaints about this appear in this book, but rather stress is laid upon their virtuous conduct in going over to help against the enemy, and their fighting for land they themselves would never inherit. Perhaps no part of Joshua's army was more thankful for the end of the warfare than they were, for this meant, as we will see later, they could return to their families.

Without attempting to go through the details of the areas here described, we might point out some matters which are interesting. It will be noticed that the boundary of the eastern portion is first defined - the River Arnon on the south, Mount Hermon in the north, the river Jordan on the west extending to the borders of the Dead Sea, but the eastern border is not clearly described except that it extended as far as the territories of Sihon and Og, the latter being the largest. We cannot but be surprised at how small was the area to be possessed. Doubtless much less than that promised to Abraham, or that possessed by Solomon. Some think it was only about one hundred miles broad and about one hundred and eighty miles long, so its importance was not due to its extent. Likewise, we are surprised that on the western side of Jordan no less than thirty one kings reigned, whereas the eastern territory had only two kings, Sihon and Og. These latter rulers must have been by far the most powerful at that time. Great changes had taken place in the Land from the time when Abraham pitched his tent in it. One of these was the great increase in its population, for it would appear that he encountered few cities if any in his travels, nor do we read of any walled or fortified towns in his time. Its ability to produce sufficient food for such numbers of people speaks well for its fertility, and reminds us that it was in truth "a land flowing with milk and honey".

While the conflict is raging it is not easy to assess the extent of its results, but when all is over and calm follows, then a proper survey of the wonder of its success can be apprehended. It is good for those who lead the saints to occasionally look over the triumphs they have achieved, not in order to boast of their own performance, but rather to recognise what the Lord has done. We should never let our failure to accomplish what we had hoped to do, close our eyes to what the Lord has wrought.

DIVIDING THE LAND (ch. 13:1-ch. 19:51)

MUCH LAND YET TO BE POSSESSED (13:1-6)

In this chapter we enter into a new phase in this book. Until now the great theme has been the mastery of the many Canaanite kings and the capture of their cities, but in this section the stress is upon the location of the various tribes in the Land, and the boundaries of their territories. Before giving us the divisions of the Land we are told of the Lord's message to Joshua. "Thou art old" were words which must have sunk deeply into his soul, nevertheless, he makes no complaint nor does he ask for an extension of his days. He is reconciled to the fact that his days of warfare are over, and that he is being allowed to enter a period of rest before he expires. Unlike Moses, who appointed his successor before he died, there is not a hint here of Joshua commissioning any one to fill his shoes, nor were they ever filled. Some have thought that this was a failing on his part, and that it accounts for the many failings in the early Judges period, but, on the other hand, it could be that he did a work which was never to be repeated, and in a sense was unique. We are not surprised that the years of conflict with the Canaanites had taken their toll and drained much of his physical strength. He was like many in retirement, who before it were so absorbed in their activities as to be almost unconscious of their weakness, but when they relaxed and the pressure was lifted they suddenly realised that they were as weak as their age implied. Later we learn that he was spared a long time after this (ch. 23:1), but during this period he lived in retirement and seemed to take no public part in the Nation.

It was never God's intention that Israel should be clustered together in one corner of the Land, but rather that Canaan should be occupied in its entirety. Before detailing the inheritance granted to each tribe, a list is given of those parts of the Land still in the hands of the enemy. As we have already noticed, the cities of the Philistines and their lords remained untouched. While mentioning these districts yet to be possessed, Joshua gave the people some idea of the extent of their inheritance. The four points of the compass are viewed, but particularly the north and south. Although the back of the enemy was broken, the inhabitants remained, so there was still much fighting to be done. Particular attention is paid to the Philistines, who had not been subdued at this time. Neither in the times of the Judges, nor in the days of Saul were they conquered, but David had the honour of becoming their master. Already two tribes and a half tribe had received their portion during the time of Moses, so past victories could be recalled which were no small encouragement in the new situation. One sad feature of the occupied territory was that the original inhabitants of the Land were not exterminated, but lived amongst the Israelites. This sparing of those who were doomed to destruction was not only contrary to God's command, but was also a potential danger in that their evil ways could be copied by God's people. It was only a matter of time until this in fact was the sad case.

Another tribe, Levi, had received its inheritance; this was not in one area, but scattered throughout the Land. The details of the cities given to it will be noticed later, but in passing it is remarkable that no less than four times we are told that its portion was distinct from all the rest of the tribes. Although much of the service of the Levites was associated with the Tabernacle, yet they were not allowed to dwell in its precincts, but were spread over every corner of the Land. No matter how remotely situated the dwelling place of any Israelite may have been, he could find a Levite in his tribal territory. These servants of God were a constant reminder to the people that there was a dwelling place which the Almighty owned as His abode, and that He would meet the needs of those who served in connection with it. Their portion was not so many acres of the Land, although they did have some fields, but rather the offerings to Jehovah made by fire were their inheritance.

In recounting the victories of Moses on the eastern side of Jordan, the writer reminds us that when defeating the princes of Midian, the diviner, Balaam, who was sought by Balak to curse Israel, was slain by the sword. Apparently, after his failure to curse Israel, he went to the Midianites who had joined Moab at that time, and fell along with them when the evil of Baal-Peor was being avenged.

Joshua, like his master, Moses, was not allowed to see all accomplished which he had in his heart. It would have been his delight to have seen the people of God settled each in his inheritance. The same limitations are often the lot of spiritual leaders when they, too, come to the end of their work. However, Joshua had made a grand beginning by capturing the many cities and defeating their kings, thus opening the way to the possessions which were promised. Nothing can be more important for any leader than to have a grasp of the extent of the spiritual inheritance that God has promised to His own. Paul, one of the great leaders, was ever burdened that those he was leaving behind should apprehend the length, breadth, depth, and height of the great mystery. The unsearchable riches which he was allowed to spread among the Gentiles, were treasures of wisdom and knowledge which he longed all the saints to apprehend. Every true leader puts as vividly as possible before those whom he leads, the vastness of their portion in Christ, even though, as in the case of Moses, he may not be spared to see them enter into it.

LAND ALREADY POSSESSED (13:7-33)

Another feature of Joshua seen at this time, and one which should be copied by all who care for the saints, was his recalling of past victories as an encouragement to future achievements. By going over in detail the area allotted to the two tribes and the half tribe, he was not only stating facts, but letting the Nation see that the prospects which lay before them were not an idle dream, but a glorious possibility.

There is some truth in what we sing, "Each victory will help you some other to win." We could become over-occupied with past failings until we could scarcely rise above them, but though we can learn from them, brooding on them continually can be very discouraging.

Without underestimating the strength of the enemy, and the difficulties which must be encountered in possessing the Land, Joshua spoke not only of the areas conquered but of the mighty kings destroyed. In mentioning these he includes among them the deadly enemy, Baalam, the false prophet who, more than any other, hurt the people of God. The outcome of his advice to Balak led to the mingling of the Israelites with the idolatrous practices of the Moabites, and this in turn brought the plague of the Lord which left twenty four thousand of Israel dead. Part of the ministry of elders involves exposing evil influences, and warning the saints of the solemn consequences of responding to them, both for those who are influenced and for those who would dare to defile the assembly of God.

PRINCIPLES OF APPORTIONMENT (14:1-5)

Having reminded the people of the tribes which had already received their inheritance by the hand of Moses, Joshua and Eleazar the priest proceeded to divide by lot the inheritance amongst the remaining nine tribes and a half tribe. Although Levi was not allotted any specific area, nevertheless there were still twelve portions in the entire inheritance. This came about by the tribe of Joseph being given a double portion, so that instead of Joseph we have his two sons Manasseh and Ephraim taking his place. Only half of the former tribe had to be accommodated in the remaining land, for already the other half had been settled on the East of Jordan. It would appear that the two halves of this tribe were not directly opposite to each other, with only the Jordan between them, for the territory given by Moses to the first half seems to be further north than the portion here given by Joshua. It was sad enough that some of the tribes desired to settle on the east side of the river, but sadder still that even in one tribe there should be this division. The people of the half tribe which chose the well-watered pasture land, appeared to have valued it more than they did the unity of the tribe. This is a solemn reminder of the power of material possessions in influencing our choice; because of them we may do things which are contrary to what would be normally expected. It will be recalled that Lot likewise valued the well-watered plains more than he valued the friendship of his uncle, Abraham.

The idea of allocating to each tribe his portion, appears a strange arrangement to our minds. Seeing all were Israelites, why not let them all live together as one great family, and forget who were their original fathers? However, we must remember that even in the wilderness the tribes were distinguished and allocated their respective positions around the Tabernacle. We have to own that later tribal rivalry showed its ugly head, and even went so far as to develop into conflict. The culmination of this evil was seen during the days of the kings, when Judah and Benjamin became separated from the other tribes. There was, no doubt great wisdom in fixing the portion of each tribe, for this meant that those fighting to possess it knew it would be theirs when the battle was over. Certainly, God never intended the allotment given to each of the tribes to be the cause of their division, but alas, what should have been for their welfare became a snare to them! Had the Land been given to the people as a whole, the outcome might well have been that only a portion of it would have been occupied, and the host of Israel content to be clustered together in a small part of it.

This great responsibility of apportioning the Land was not something that Joshua would undertake alone. The choice for each tribe was not a matter for him, but for the Lord to decide, so Eleazar the priest is brought into it, for he would be the most suited man in Israel to cast the lots, and by so doing obtain the mind of the Lord. Doubtless this priest had been at the first distribution conducted by Moses, so this other one to be done on the same pattern would present no difficulty to him. Seeing the lot was decided by the Lord neither Eleazar nor Joshua could have been blamed by any who was not satisfied with the portion granted to him. It would appear that after the territory was allocated to Judah and Ephraim there was a pause for some time before the rest of the Land was divided.

THE CLAIM OF CALEB (14:6-15)

When the territory of Judah was about to be distributed, the head of this tribe, Caleb, put in his plea for that portion which had been promised him by Moses. In a sense, his allotment had been settled some forty five years earlier, for he had been one of the two spies who brought back a good report of the Land, and did so against ten of his fellow spies. It is most interesting to consider the three notable men - Joshua, Eleazar, and Caleb - who met together on this occasion. All of them had been in Egypt, all had passed through the Red Sea, all had travelled through the wilderness and had witnessed their fellows being slain by the Lord. It will be recalled that Joshua and Caleb saw the wrath of the Lord fall upon their ten fellow spies, when they died by the plague before the Lord (Num 14:37), and that Eleazar also had the painful experience of witnessing the death of his two elder brothers, when the fire of the Lord consumed them as they offered their strange incense before the Lord (Lev 10:1 - 2). Likewise all of them passed through Jordan. Some forty five years had elapsed since Caleb had first set foot on what was at length to be his inheritance. His preservation and healthy faculties were little short of a miracle. Apparently, he had taken part in the wars of Canaan, and was feeling still fit for battle. The giants which he had seen when he spied out the Land had not grown any larger in his estimation, for he was raring to attack them and so to prove that they were only bread ready to be consumed. Much stress is laid upon the fact that what he was seeking was promised to him because he had "wholly followed the Lord". His faith in the One who had destroyed Pharaoh and his army at the Red Sea, remained unshaken when he returned from the excursion of the Land, and now, after so many years, it remained as firm as ever.

The city, Hebron, here said to be given to Caleb, was not given him by lot, for it was his by promise many years before these lots were cast. The days when he walked upon the slopes on which it stood was the time when his portion was settled. Often he must have dreamed about what it would be like to dwell in that good Land, and the years of sojourning in the wilderness must have been a sore trial for him to endure. Not only did he need to be spared through that rough and arduous journey, but he needed to retain his mental and physical strength in order to enter and enjoy what he had earlier prized. Like Moses, his natural force was not abated nor was his courage daunted. Although he travelled for the most of forty years with a multitude of unbelievers, yet he retained and confessed with boldness his faith in the Lord. These many years must have brought great changes to the city and its surroundings, but he had not altered his opinion as to its worth, nor did he ask for any other part of the Land. Evidently it was no easy feat to capture Hebron, for we learn from Judges that Joshua's army, along with Caleb and his younger half-brother Othniel, were all engaged in its capture. This latter proved to be the champion of the day, for he led the attack and took it, and obtained a bride for his achievement. Caleb had promised to give his daughter to the man who would take Hebron. It turned out to be his half-brother who did this, so the bride he obtained was his niece. (See Jud 1:10 - 13.)

This story of allotting the Land sparkles with lessons for all responsible brethren to learn. To begin with, it has to be ever borne in mind that all believers are not given the same gift, and what is more important, that just as the

Land was divided by lot, so the Lord is sovereign as to what each should have. He still divides according as He will, so we must accept His verdict and make no attempt to change what cannot be altered. Elders should ever be on the look out for those indications in younger believers of what is the purpose of the Lord for them. They should not become jealous if someone younger than themselves apprehends truth in a fuller way than they have been able to do. Furthermore, they must take account of handicaps which some have had because of the failures of others, and allow for late developers who really only enter into their inheritance when much of their lives is over. Jacob, the father of the nation, was an example of one who ripened spiritually in his closing years. The true leader neither rejects the young nor despises the older. Some, like Caleb and his possession, regret that the treasures of truth they now enjoy were not enjoyed by them in their early days.

Honouring earlier promises, even those not personally made, is a vital quality in a true elder. Joshua never questioned the claim that Caleb made, but agreed to it as though he himself had decided it. Sometimes the oversight of an assembly inherits promises made to members of it by elders who are now gone; these should, whenever possible, be fulfilled.

THE INHERITANCE OF JUDAH (15:1-63)

The first part of the Land to be divided by lot was the portion of Judah. To this tribe was allocated the most southerly as well as the most important territory of Canaan. The preference given to this tribe may well have been because, according to the prophecy of Jacob, there would rise up out of it the monarchy in Israel. Simeon, who according to Jacob's prophecy was to be scattered in Israel, was given his portion amongst this tribe. Though he was an older son in the family, yet he lost his preference to Judah, not only because of the crime committed by himself, but also because his descendants lost heavily in the wilderness and were the smallest in numbers of all the tribes. Indeed, their numbers at this time were less than a third of that of Judah. A description of Judah's borders is here given, and this extended to the Land of Edom on the south, to the Dead Sea on the east, to the border of Benjamin's portion on the north and to the Mediterranean Sea on the west. In the after history of Israel, whether we think of the times of David and the kings, or the times of Christ, this area was of great importance. Jerusalem, though at times reckoned to be in the territory of Benjamin, was in some respects part of Judah. In fact it seemed to straddle the border between the two tribes.

Although the story of Caleb has already been given in ch. 14, it is raised again in this chapter. However it is not now so much the allotment of his portion but the capturing of it that is here referred to. Apparently, the city of Debir was a challenge to him and his men, so he offered his daughter as a reward for the man who could take it. The hero who did so was his own brother, Othniel, so to him he gave Achsah his daughter and she became the wife of her uncle, or perhaps her half-uncle, for Caleb and Othniel were only half-brothers. When she looked at the city and its suburbs she noticed that a supply of water was lacking, so in a most respectful manner she dismounted from her ass and put in her plea for some springs. Her father acceded to her request by giving her the upper and nether springs.

Following this account of the allotting of the Land to the tribe of Judah, we have a list of some one hundred and fifty cities which were included in it. Many of the names in this list became famous, such as Jerusalem, Ziklag, Hebron, and Carmel, but others are unnoticed in after history. Notwithstanding the fact that according to ch. 10, Joshua captured Jerusalem and slew its king, yet we are told that the Jebusites, who must have re-taken it, dwelt in it. Not until the days of David was it fully in the hands of the Israelites. This brief statement at the close of the chapter explains why so much fighting had to be done in the days of the Judges. Although Joshua and his army took so much of the Land, yet the cities conquered were not possessed by the people, so naturally the former inhabitants returned to their abodes, and attempted to fortify themselves against the invaders.

Leaders should learn from Joshua that those worthy of positions of responsibility should have these allotted to them. He himself was not of the tribe of Judah, but this did not influence his choice of giving it first place. Overcoming favouritism and natural relationships is vital in assembly life. The Lord's mind must ever be supreme, and even when it may not be exactly what we would naturally desire, yet it must be owned and obeyed. While Joshua delineated the exact territory to this tribe, they did not receive it without fighting for it. In granting responsibilities by the oversight of an assembly, it has to be borne in mind that the receivers have their part to play, in which they will prove their worthiness for the position given.

Just as in the case of Achsah, some may not be satisfied with the portion allotted to them but will seek something additional to it; in such circumstances careful heed should be paid to their requests, and these should be granted when reasonable. For example, if one were put in charge of a Bible-class and not given suitable accommodation for it, he would have just cause for putting his requirements before the elders. However blessed an assembly may be with spiritual elders, those they lead do not receive their spiritual inheritance from the hands of men. Believers in all generations have to contend against the powers of darkness if they are to obtain and retain their allotted portion. Truth learned in the school of conflict and trial is usually held with firmer grip by those who have struggled to obtain it. Quite often those who are as it were spoon-fed, fail to value as they should what is handed to them. The true leader will, like Joshua, set a good example, but will not fail to stress to his followers the importance of their own individual exercise in obtaining what the Lord has purposed for them to enjoy.

THE PORTION OF THE TRIBE OF JOSEPH
(16:1-17:18)

Having settled the bounds of the tribe of Judah, Joshua proceeds to map out the territory allotted to the tribe of Joseph. Because the birthright was Joseph's his descendants had a double portion, so in these chapters we are told of the lots of Ephraim and Manasseh. Jacob had indicated in his blessing of Joseph's sons that they would be heads of tribes, and that the younger son, Ephraim, would have the pre-eminence. The birthright, however, remained with Manasseh, so he had two portions, one on either side Jordan. The combined numbers of Ephraim and Manasseh exceeded any other tribe in Israel, so they claimed a large inheritance. The area given to Ephraim was in the centre of the Land, and included some of the most famous places mentioned in Scripture, such as Shiloh, Jericho, Bethel, Mount Ebal, and Mount Gerizim. That given to Manasseh was both hilly and wooded, and was more northerly. For reasons we are not told, some of the cities given to this tribe were in the territory allotted to Issachar and Asher. Amongst them are Bethshean, Dor, Endor and Megiddo. Some of these places became famous in later history. The latter especially was the scene of many battles, and, in a future day, will again be the centre of conflict. In our chapter and in Judges 1 a city in Ephraim is specially mentioned, which apparently put up stiff resistance, for in both passages we are told that "Ephraim drave not out the Canaanites which dwelt in Gezer; but the Canaanites dwelt among them". This city appears to have been of strategic importance and was captured by Joshua in his earlier campaign, but, as happened in other places, the inhabitants returned to it, and although put to task-work, refused to be driven out completely. Notwithstanding their great numbers and high claims, the Ephraimites proved their weakness in this vital place. In this respect they were no better than the tribe of Judah, and the city of Jerusalem, for they also could not drive out the inhabitants; here the people were made slaves, whereas no such claim was made in the former story.

In allotting the inheritance of Manasseh the problem reappeared regarding the portion of Zelophehad who died without having any sons. This matter had already been dealt with by Moses in Num 26:33 and 36:1 - 12. The normal right to heirship was in the male line, but in this test case it was commanded by the Lord that if the daughters married within their own tribe they would receive the inheritance of their father. Of the ten portions allotted to Manasseh five were given to these daughters.

Just as Judah and Ephraim had proved unable to expel the Canaanites, so also did Manasseh fail, and only when strong did he manage to put them to task-work. With the Israelites being compelled to live side by side with these idolaters, there was ever the temptation that their evil ways would prove harmful and contagious as time passed. Alas the later history records that this was the case! Many years after this Jeroboam set one of his centres of idolatry in Bethel, a place which was in the territory of Joseph.

It is most difficult when various portions are being distributed to satisfy all the recipients. In this case, while the lots were directed by the Lord, yet Joshua was the one who had to listen to the complaints. His own tribe, Ephraim, which had waxed strong and had become a great people, felt that it had not been given a large enough territory. Possibly his influence in favouring his own tribe had been suspected, but even if this were possible, he was too spiritual to stoop to such a selfish move. The complaint of these men was answered with great tact and a tinge of irony. They were told there was plenty of room on the mountain slopes, where the task of removing the wood would be repaid by the revenue received from its sale. The implication was obvious: if they were the great people they claimed to be, then there was a golden opportunity to prove it. Apparently they were between the hills with their trees, and the valleys with the iron chariots. Neither land was going to be easily mastered but a challenge faced them, so instead of complaining they should be up and doing. The Lord who had proved so strong for Joshua in his wars was well able to strengthen them for the task involved.

In these two chapters which we have looked at there are some lessons to be learned that we might be slow to notice. Not the least of these is the evidence of weakness in dealing with the inhabitants of the Land. We know that the Lord directed that these should be utterly destroyed, but the Israelites spared them. In our case these enemies represent the evil forces which would keep us from enjoying our portion in Christ. We are meant to hold our ground, and to defend ourselves against all attempts of the powers of darkness to rob us of our inheritance. For this very purpose we have been equipped with our armour. It is to our shame that we have to confess that instead of the victory being ours it is the enemy who wins the day. The temptation to compromise with the enemy, and as it were put him to tribute, is present with us. Many feel relieved at even partial success, for they claim it is better than total defeat. It is so, but again it is not what God intended.

The rights of our sisters, as illustrated in the daughters of Zelophehad, must ever be present to our minds. While they are not allowed to engage in public ministry, just as these girls were not expected to be in the army, yet they have their portion. Most are agreed that Mary at the feet of Jesus enjoyed a part which gave her an insight into His mind to an extent which even surpassed some of His disciples. There were bounds set to these daughters, just as there are restrictions put upon sisters, but these did not prevent them entering into the inheritance of their father. The men of their own tribe who married them found not only brides but territorial wealth as well. The spiritual wealth of many assemblies has been increased by those sisters in them who have taken hold of the treasures of truth passed on to them by older brethren.

A further lesson to be heeded is seen in the boastful spirit of the tribe of Ephraim. Not a few would like more place in the assembly, and feel that their importance is not being recognised. To such we can adopt the attitude of Joshua. There is much scope for development in every area, so let those who claim they have strength go to battle and prove their worth. The wise leader knows how to meet pride in such a way that he turns it into action. Many over-estimate their abilities and think others are only school-boys in the work of God, yet when put to the test they prove to be just as weak as other men. While we are humbled at the smallness of the numbers in some assemblies, yet we must not think because the company has large numbers in fellowship that it is necessarily in possession of great spiritual wealth.

THE ALLOTMENTS OF THE REMAINING SEVEN TRIBES (18:1-19:51)

There appears to have been a break in the distribution of the Land after the portions of Judah and Joseph were settled. The remaining lots were decided at the Tabernacle, but not until a survey had been taken of that part which had yet to be allocated. Without any details being given, we are told that the Tabernacle at this time was erected at Shiloh. According to Deut 12, the choice of the place where God would place His name was made by Him alone, so we must conclude that He had indicated to Eleazar, possibly by the Urim and Thummim, that this location was the place which He had chosen. The site, being in the centre of the Land, was an ideal one. The Tabernacle may not have remained there all the time, but we do know that it was still there in Samuel's day. At the beginning of Solomon's reign it was sited at Gibeon, and possibly remained there until it was taken down and stored in the Temple. The removal from it of the Ark in the days of Eli signified that the glory of God's presence had departed from it, and that it had been forsaken by Him as His dwelling place. Nevertheless, the Lord must have retained some respect for it, for sacrifices offered on its altar were accepted by Him, and during a visit to it by Solomon, He appeared unto him there.

As for the name Shiloh, which means "peace" or "rest", it was first used by Jacob in his blessing of Judah, where it most likely refers to Christ who is the "Prince of peace", and the giver of rest Joshua may have adopted it from the song of the patriarch, and applied it to the site where the Tabernacle was erected. Possibly no place in the Land bore this name before this time, and if so, he must have deemed it to be an appropriate appellation for it. His reason for this may well have been that the Tabernacle, which had been on the move from the time when it was first made, had now found a more permanent resting place. Most likely around it would have been pitched the tents of those in Israel who had not as yet obtained their possession. Be that as it may, on this occasion Joshua summoned the entire camp and admonished the people regarding the urgency of proceeding with the warfare involved in possessing the remainder of the Land. Their success in obtaining the southern area, instead of encouraging them to venture into the northern territory, seems to have caused them to settle down and feel content, as though this were the only part to be possessed; but their slackness was rebuked by their leader, who had a more ambitious outlook than his followers. The fact that the whole congregation had been called to assemble in the presence of God, marked the occasion as one of singular importance.

Seven more tribes had, as yet, received no inheritance, so the vital business in hand was to decide what portion each of these tribes would be given. In order to do this, it was necessary that a survey of the remainder of the Land should be carried out and a map of this should be drawn up. This territory was divided into seven parts, and then lots cast so as to settle which portion each remaining tribe would be given. The task of finding out the borders and the sizes of these sections was entrusted to twenty one men, three from each of the seven tribes. Apparently, all travelled together, for it was most important that there should be agreement as to what particular area would constitute a fair portion for any one tribe to possess. It has to be remembered that when reaching their decision as to this, none of these men knew which part was to be given to his own tribe. All this was designed, no doubt, to prevent as far as possible any complaints arising when the lots were later cast.

This survey of the Land is the third one of which we read. There was the first spying of it in the days of Moses, when twelve men, one from each tribe, went over Jordan and saw the walled cities and the giants; the result of this was the disaster of Kadesh-Barnea; then, when Jordan was again reached, Joshua sent two spies to view Jericho; and here, in this passage, he has another survey taken. However, this last one differed from the previous two, in that it involved the mapping out of the territory, noting its characteristics, and particularly marking its natural boundaries so that any one of its seven portions would, though different in area, be a suitable possession for any tribe to inherit. Spying of this nature must of necessity have involved serious risks, for the identity of the Israelite men could not be concealed, more especially when in a group of twenty one. Possibly the dread and fear that the Lord's doings in the south had produced in the hearts of the people of the Land, may have prevented them from attacking these men.

When the survey was completed, it was discovered that the portions which had already been allocated to Judah and Joseph were much larger than any of the seven portions which remained, so it was decided that the lot for the tribe of Simeon would be part of the area originally given to Judah, and that Benjamin's lot was to be between Judah and Ephraim. This mingling of Simeon's lot with that of Judah was the fulfilment of the threat in Jacob's song concerning Simeon, which stated that his tribe would be scattered amongst the other tribes. Thus both Judah and Ephraim had to give up cities to their neighbouring tribes. It is of interest to note that Jerusalem was one of the cities given to Benjamin, but being on the border of Judah's lot, it at times is viewed as though it belonged to the latter tribe. Other cities of interest in the list of this tribe are Jericho, Bethel, Ophrah, Gibeon and Gibeah. The two Sauls of Scripture both belonged to it. There was a time when because of the evil at Gibeah it was almost wiped out, yet it must have revived to some degree, and had the honour of producing Israel's first king, and what was more important, the great apostle to the Gentiles. Paul could boast of being one of its number. The tribe of Simeon, too, had some interesting places granted to it; among these were Beersheba, Ziklag and Rimmon.

The territory given to Zebulun was apparently entirely inland, for in the details of its borders there is no mention of either river or sea. Though unknown in the days of Joshua, the town of Nazareth in which the Lord was brought up was situated within its borders. Of interest too is Gath-hepher, the birth-place of the prophet Jonah, so the charge made in the days of Christ that "no prophet came out of Galilee" was entirely false.

In the territory of Issachar was the famous city of Jezreel where Ahab had his palace, and where Baal was worshipped. Another spot in this tribe's portion was Shunem where abode the widow whose son was raised by Elisha.

Asher and Napthtali were neighbours and also constituted part of what was known in the NT as Galilee. The lake which also bore this name was surrounded by towns much visited by the Lord, and the scene of many of His mighty works. Apparently these northern tribes were greatly despised by the Jews and regarded by them as dark heathen, but the light shed abroad by Christ turned many of these degraded people, including most of the apostles, into testimony-bearers, not only to the Nation but to the whole world. Anna, who came to the Temple when the Lord was being presented by His parents and who later spoke of Him to the faithful in Jerusalem, belonged to the former tribe.

Dan was the last of the tribes to receive an inheritance. His portion was between Judah and the Land of the Philistines. These Philistines were mighty warriors who had emigrated from Egypt and had chosen one of the best parts of the Land. They were such a formidable foe that the Danites were unable to drive them out of their possession. Because of this, a large contingent of the Danites emigrated to the far north of the Land, where they planted a city and called it Dan. This is why the extent of the country from north to south is described as "from Dan to Beer-sheba". The Sidonians whose land they possessed were no easy prey, but were not so formidable as the Philistines. Perhaps the mighty Samson, who was of this tribe, restored to it some of its lost honour. Already we have noted that the inheritance of Manasseh was divided, and now another tribe became divided although allotted a single portion, but in this case the new area possessed was not chosen under the Lord's direction. At the end of the book of Judges we learn that these northern settlers were foremost in Israel in turning to idolatry.

We are somewhat amazed at the acceptance by each tribe without controversy of the portion allotted to it. This, as we have pointed out, was due to the wisdom of Joshua in allowing the Lord to make the decision as to where each tribe should locate. It remained from this time onward for each one of them to possess its own possession. In the former wars, the entire army was involved under Johua's leadership, so victory was assured, but now each tribe has to do its own warring and thereby prove for itself the power of the Lord. In ch. 11:23 we read that "Joshua took the whole land, and that the Land rested from war"; here (19:51) we learn that this same Land has been distributed, so the second great task of this renowned leader had been accomplished. In spite of the slaughter of the kings and the destruction of the cities of Canaan, it would appear that the population remaining was a formidable obstacle in the way of Israel possessing the Land, and enjoying to the full the inheritance it had been promised.

Not until all others had received their portions had any reference been made as to where Joshua himself should dwell. If any man deserved a choice allottment it was the one who had conducted the entire campaign, and did so in his old age. Notwithstanding all that he had accomplished, he was not allowed to select his portion but was given it by the commandment of the Lord. He was granted Timnath-serah - a city in his own tribe, but one of no importance or of any natural fertile qualities. Indeed it would appear that he had to build the city, so there was little or nothing to begin with. In accepting this as his portion he displayed the humility of his mind, and the unselfishness of his heart. Most army generals retire into luxury, and are not only provided with the best but are so enriched that their posterity will know no want. Joshua began as the servant of Moses, and he was content to end in humble circumstances; in this he is typical of the One who began His life on earth in a manger and ended it on a cross.

The lessons in these chapters are many, but we will touch upon only a few of the most obvious. The

Tabernacle erected in Shiloh reminds us of the importance of the divine centre, where the Lord has placed His name, and where His presence is realised. At its door all important decisions were made under His guidance. In our day this corresponds to the assembly of God gathered to His name. Where such should be planted must be always left for Him to decide. He alone can provide the material to form a testimony, and only by His help can it be maintained. In this age we do not cast lots, nor have we anything equivalent to the Urim and Thummim, nevertheless we are not without guidance, for we have the complete word of God. Its authority must ever be supreme, and its judgment final.

Those who lead the saints should have a deep exercise to see that each of them be given the portion of responsibility for which he has been fitted by the Lord. Just as Joshua charged Israel to possess the Land, so believers should be exhorted to acquire their share of the inheritance which the Lord has purposed for them to enjoy. In claiming this there will be conflict with the powers of darkness, but the Lord can help, even when His people feel that they are no match for those who rise up against them. There was a part for all in Israel, so no tribe was allowed to claim the Land for itself . There is ever the danger of the more powerful and the more able brethren monopolising all the responsibilities, but the true leader will make sure that every one has a part and that none is despised.

Sometimes it transpires that some have more responsibility in hand than they can cope with, so just as Judah and Ephraim had to surrender part of their original allocation to other tribes, so these have to give to others what they cannot manage themselves. In the early days in an assembly one or two may have to carry most of the burden of it, but later, if they are wise, they will allow others who have developed by the grace of the Lord to help them carry the load.

Those who have been instrumental in establishing an assembly, and who are leaders in it, will be tempted to expect great regard from those whom they have enriched. In this they may be disappointed, but the truly humble man will, like Joshua, think little of self and be content to enjoy whatever the Lord is pleased to give him. Joshua could have said to the people, "But for me, you would not own a sod in Canaan, so I have the right to dwell in the choicest place in the Land", but no such spirit prevailed in him. The hallmark of a great man is that he foregoes his rights.

There will ever be those amongst the saints who, like the Danites, will feel that their lot has been in most difficult circumstances. The temptation is great for such to seek, even at the cost of division, an easier portion. Even in Gospel work there are areas more difficult than others, but this does not mean that they should be shunned. The arch-enemy holds on to his choicest treasures, and will not yield them up without putting up stiff resistance. We have to remember that often what can be obtained at little cost is of little value, whereas the most precious possessions can be acquired only at great cost.

ENJOYING THE LAND (ch. 20:1-ch. 24:33)

THE CITIES OF REFUGE (20:1-9)

At the time of the distribution of the Land another matter had to be settled, for Moses had given instructions that out of the many cities potentially possessed, six were to be set apart as cities of refuge. In Ex 21, Num 35, and Deut 19 he had given clear guidance regarding these cities and their use. They were havens to which the manslayer could flee if he had killed someone accidentally. The Lord spoke to Joshua concerning this important matter, and instructed him to appoint these cities. It was the duty of the "avenger of blood" (the *goel*, or "redeemer") to avenge the blood of his near relatives, so if one of these was killed unintentionally, the slayer was to be put to death. However, his execution was avoided if he fled to one of these chosen cities. Whatever may be our thoughts of the avenger's severe treatment, the fact remains that it taught the Nation the sanctity of human life. Possibly because of this law we never read of anyone having to avail himself of one of these cities. Many so-called accidents are the result of carelessness, and could be avoided if more thought was given to the risks which lead to them. In Israel there was no doubt about the penalty involved if a life were lost, so the dread of this played a part in establishing proper behaviour, especially when something entailing risk was being done.

These places of shelter were only for those who killed unwittingly, but provided no refuge for the wilful murderer. He could flee thither if he liked, but he would then be tried and executed for his crime. In spite of the primitive conditions which prevailed in those times, the Lord enlightened His people as to the difference between manslaughter and murder.

Two important factors had to be borne in mind in selecting these cities; one was their location, the other was their accessibility. These requirements were met in that three of them were on each side of Jordan so even if the river was in flood the manslayer would have no necessity to cross over it. Great care had to be taken that no obstacle was on the way which led to any of these cities, lest the fleer should be overtaken before he could reach its refuge. In appointing (the word is "sanctifying") these cites, Joshua was careful that on the west side of the river he selected Kedesh in Naphtali, which was in the north; Shechem in Ephraim, which was in the centre of the Land; and Kirjath-arba in Judah, which was in the south, so these three were well distributed and were within reach of all on that side of Jordan. On the east side, Bezer in Reuben was in the south; Ramoth in Gilead was in the tribe of Gad and in the middle; and Golan in Bashan was in the tribe of Manasseh and in the north so again the three sites were well situated for their intended purpose. It is important to note that all six cites of refuge were Levitical cities, so their inhabitants were associated with the Tabernacle, and because of this were well acquainted with the requirements of God.

These cities were a mild form of imprisonment, for those who fled to them were confined within their gates, so were cut off from all who were dear to them and from their normal means of living. Not until the death of the high-priest could they venture into freedom, and return to their own inheritance. Why his death should be the occasion for this is not easy to see, except that his death was such a national calamity and would cause such widespread grief that all other deaths would be disregarded. Some have suggested that when the priest died, being the representative of the Nation, all died in him, so this ended all rights of the kinsman to avenge blood. Whatever be the basis of God's provision for Israel, we are clear that for us who believe there was a time when we were awakened to realise our danger and when we "fled for refuge", and are now safe for ever. Our forerunner and High-Priest has entered within the veil and is alive forevermore.

There are occasions when, even in our day, some of our brethren can be injured in a spiritual sense, and while not slain as to the body, they are nevertheless so wounded in soul as to be all but dead. The idea of taking vengeance by those who support such victims should never arise. Those who have a care for the saints should be quick to find out if the blows struck were intentional or were merely accidental. It is all too easy for any of us to assume that something said was deliberately aimed at us, when in fact the speaker had no such thought in his mind. Many have nursed wounds which if they had known the true facts would never have been felt. On the other hand, let us not under-estimate the seriousness of deliberately "slaughtering" any brother, for by so doing we could not only spoil his usefulness but could bring down God's judgment upon ourselves. If God in a past day held sacred the physical life of His people, we can be sure He has in this age no less respect for the welfare of the spiritual life of His own. As for taking vengeance on our enemies, this too is not allowed, but must be left to Him who has said, "Vengeance is mine".

THE INHERITANCE OF THE LEVITES (21:1-45)

Throughout the book of Joshua we have been reminded that the Levites had no inheritance in Israel, but that the Lord was their inheritance. (See chs. 13:33; 14:3; and 18:7.) This did not deprive them of a dwelling place, nor did it degrade them to the level of paupers. Their portion was indeed a rich one, for almost one fifth of the income of the Nation was given to them. Because their duties were mainly in connection with the Tabernacle, we would expect them to have been located near its precincts, but God thought otherwise, and scattered them over the entire Land. This scattering had been prophesied by Jacob but it was tempered with honour, for what their father Levi had lost through his cruelty, his descendants had gained because of their faithfulness in a dark day.

The tribe of Levi was by far the smallest in number of the tribes, so had an inheritance been given in proportion to its size, it would have been exceedingly small. Even though its sons were counted from a month old, and not twenty years old as was the case with the other tribes, yet the total only reached twenty three thousand. One explanation for the fewness of its numbers is that, because of the special work entrusted to the sons of this tribe only pure descendants from Levi were counted, whereas there could have been included in the census of the other tribes, many who were attached to them as servants, or many who are called "the mixed multitude". While it was settled even before the day that the Israelites crossed the Jordan that provision would be made for the Levites, this could not be allocated to them until the cities of each tribe had been assigned. When the Land was divided by Joshua, then the Levites approached the high-priest, Eleazar, and asked for the cities which they had been promised by Moses. There would have been serious injustice in the distribution of the Land, if they had to continue dwelling in tents while their brethren were enjoying the comforts of good housing. They, and no doubt Joshua and the elders in Israel, realised that the time was opportune for this matter to be settled, so a total of forty eight cites was given to them. This was on average four from each of the other tribes.

It is interesting to note that the Kohathites, some of whom were priests the descendants of Aaron, had their cities in the southern and central areas, so were reasonably convenient to Shiloh where the Tabernacle was at this time, and not too far from the Temple which was later erected in Zion. God not only considered the needs of Shiloh, but also foresaw the time when He would place His name in Jerusalem, and where those who would then serve in His house would be suitably accommodated.

The first city to be given to the priests was Hebron in the territory of Judah. Already we have seen that this was the chosen inheritance of Caleb, and that it was taken from the descendants of a man called Arba who was the greatest man among the Anakims. Here we learn that this prized place was transferred to the Kohathites. It must have been no small sacrifice for Caleb to leave the city and dwell in the surrounding hill-country. Not only had he to give up the inhabited part of it, but also the fields surrounding it, for the Levites were not only granted places to dwell in, but were also allotted Land for the grazing of their cattle. The old man seemed to be quite content with his lot, even though its centre and built up area had become, not only a city of refuge, but also a habitation of those of another tribe. Of the forty eight cities given to the Levites, there was none more interesting than Hebron, formerly called Kirjath-arba, or the fourfold city. It was possibly one of the oldest cities in Canaan, and must have been built soon after the flood. Unlike many ancient places which are now nothing but a heap of ruins, Hebron still exists, so must be one of the oldest cities in the world. Abraham dwelt in it and built an altar there. Later his wife Sarah died there, and near to it he purchased the cave of Machpelah (Gen 23) where she was buried; later he himself together with most of the patriarchs were also buried there. It would seem that this city and the surrounding hills were that part of the Land surveyed by Caleb and the other spies (Num 13). Even though it was fortified and possessed by the greatest of the giants, he had no doubt that the Lord would enable Israel to possess it. As we have seen, he was originally granted this special city as his reward for faithfulness, but now had to forfeit it to the Levites.

Apparently the Levites, being set apart for the service of God, had no part in the wars of Canaan. They entered into their inheritance without having to fight for it. The Lord had claimed them as His portion instead of the firstborn of all the Nation, so in giving them their dwellings He was simply claiming for Himself that part of the inheritance which rightly belonged to Him. Had it not been for His power and help none of the Land would have been possessed, and, strictly speaking, He was only claiming what was His own, so all those who gave up cities could say like David, "Of thine own have we given thee".

Another city of some interest in this list is Shechem, for it too appears in the former history of Israel. Jacob had sad memories of it, because it was there that Dinah was defiled, and where, because of this, his sons took vengeance on its inhabitants (Gen 34). Just as Abraham purchased the cave of Machpelah, so Jacob bought a piece of ground near to Shechem, which he later gave to Joseph. It too became a burying place for the bones of Joseph were buried there. Likewise, it was not only a city given to the Levites, but was also a city of refuge. What makes it most interesting to the saints is that the Lord met the woman at its well (John 4). The great Antitype of Joseph received His portion as He sat there, for He could say, "I have meat to eat that ye know not of" (v. 32).

After naming the forty eight cities given to the Levites, the writer of our book gives a glowing report of the Lord's doings for Israel (vv. 43 - 45). First, He gave them the Land, and they now possess it and dwell in it. Secondly, they by His help had destroyed all their enemies and were now able to rest from war. Thirdly, He had kept all His promises, even though some of them were made a long time before this. In the comparatively short period since they had crossed over Jordan, the Lord had done great things for them, and made their hearts rejoice.

The example of Joshua and Eleazar should be followed by all who have the oversight of an assembly. They, like them, should give instruction to the saints in the great matter of giving the Lord His portion. Just as the priests and the Levites were supported by the secular part of the Nation, so in this day the needs of those who devote all their time and energies to His service are met by the sacrifices of the rest of His people. In their liberal giving they are demonstrating their appreciation of what they owe to the Lord for all He has done for them. A large number of saints realise that, had they remained in their sins and lived recklessly as they did before conversion, then they would be very much poorer now, even in material things. We noted that in the selecting of these cities the Lord chose the best, so we must remember that

God gave His own choicest possession when He gave His Son, and He would desire to reproduce His own character in His children, so that they too sacrifice for Him what is dear to their hearts. We have seen how Caleb parted with Hebron, which city must have been dear to him, and we know that the father of the Nation was asked to part with his only son, so we may be sure that God still expects His people to give up what they would naturally desire to retain. When Israel drifted away from God, the Levites were neglected and had to return to ordinary labour in order to obtain their necessities; so in our day, if the hearts of the saints become cold, they become careless and rob the Lord of His portion.

THE DISMISSAL OF THE ARMY OF THE TWO TRIBES AND THE HALF TRIBE (22:1-9)

Now that the wars were over, the Land captured, and the enemies conquered, the soldiers who had fulfilled their duty in helping their brethren on the western side of Jordan to obtain their inheritance had no further necessity to remain away from their own loved ones and from their own possession. No doubt they welcomed the call of Joshua for them to assemble at Shiloh and hear his instructions regarding their departure. They were possibly parted from their families for almost seven years, so it was time they were restored to normal family life. Joshua pays tribute to their faithful and gallant service, and to their faithful obedience to the commandment of Moses, who had given them instructions regarding their passing over to help. We can be sure a warm and hero's welcome awaited them in Gilead, where their loved ones must have felt the period of their absence abnormally long. With the excitement of battle the days would pass quickly for the soldiers, but those at home had no such relief, neither had they any easy means of communication which would have enabled them to learn of the wellbeing of their loved ones. Many anxious thoughts must have passed over their minds, and possibly even fears that they would never see them again.

Three features marked Joshua's parting address to them; first, a word of praise for their steadfastness; secondly, a word of warning regarding the keeping of God's commandments; and thirdly, a word of instruction regarding the spoils which they were bringing home with them. Joshua was a man who knew when a work was well done, and was not hesitant in giving due praise to those who deserved it. Nevertheless, he has had experience with the Nation, and this had taught him that its people were ever in danger of departing from the Lord. The secret of the preservation of these tribes was love to the Lord, a love which would be expressed in the keeping of His commandments. He heaps up words in order to press home the exhortation. They were to "take diligent heed", were "charged to love the Lord", to "walk in his ways" to "keep his commandments", to "cleave unto him", and to "serve him with heart and soul".

These soldiers were not returning home empty-handed. They were laden with the spoils of their enemies, for just as the Israelites stripped Egypt of its wealth when they left for the wilderness, so these men stripped the nations of Canaan, and carried home with them wealth which they never thought they would possess. They might have been tempted to retain all these riches for themselves and their families, perhaps under the principle that they had risked their lives to obtain them, but Joshua would not have this, for he reckoned that those who remained at home had also paid a price for this wealth in that they had endured the loneliness without their sons or their husbands, so they deserved to have their share of it. The same principle was later enjoined by David who said, "As his part is that goeth down to the battle, so shall his part be that tarried by the stuff" (1 Sam 30:24).

The last sight Joshua saw before he slipped into the background, was the army from the east go away driving their cattle, and carrying home the treasures of precious metal which they had accumulated during the campaign in Canaan. All the time they were with him they had dwelt in tents, for they knew that they were not to dwell in the place where they had warred. The years spent with the western tribes must have forged bonds between them, but now these were to be severed, not only momentarily, but most likely for ever. The men of Manasseh especially must have felt the wrench, for they were parting from their fellow tribesmen. We are not told how they crossed the river Jordan, but likely the fords would have been passable except at the time of flood.

Those who carry responsibility for directing assembly matters must ever be careful to give due praise to those who sacrifice in their service for the Lord. Nothing can be more discouraging to any one who has laboured with all his might to advance the work of God, than to find those in leadership ignoring his efforts and at times finding fault that he did not do it better. Perhaps the danger of some becoming inflated has made elders hesitant to give praise to anyone. Certainly wisdom is needed, for there is the possibility of encouraging pride, and no one would wish to fan that flame. However, it is obvious that Joshua's praise on this occasion led to his strong exhortation, so this balance must ever be retained in dealing with workers - praise for what has been done, and strong warnings regarding the future.

The sharing of spiritual wealth must ever be encouraged by those who direct the saints. There are those who can gather the spoils of spiritual treasure from the word of God, and they might say to others, "Go and gather it for yourselves", but this is not always fair, for some cannot study as deeply as they would like, and are dependent upon others to bring home to them what is most precious truth, and what they value very highly. Nothing can be more stifling in the sphere of spiritual progress than for those who are able to enter into the treasures of Scripture to retain all they enjoy to themselves. Quite often those who enrich others are enriched themselves, and those who refuse to share what they have acquired become impoverished in their own souls. God arranged that those who were unable to gather the manna in the wilderness had provision made for them by those who gathered more than they needed for themselves.

THE GREAT ALTAR ED (22:10-34)

The episode of these verses may not have occurred for some time after the army of the two tribes and half tribe returned to their brethren, but being connected with their departure from the west side of Jordan it is recorded here. Already two monuments had been erected at Jordan at the time of the crossing, and now a more elaborate structure of stone was built by those who belonged to the eastern side of the river. This stone altar must have borne some resemblance to the brazen altar at Shiloh, so it possibly was hollow in the centre and raised up at the corners to represent the horns of it. Concerning the actual location of this altar there is much difference of opinion. Many believe it was on the west bank, and therefore on the side where the earlier stones were raised, but others think, and perhaps rightly, that in order to be a witness to the eastern tribes it must have been erected on their territory. Some time after it was built news of this was conveyed to the elders and priests at Shiloh. As soon as this was known the worst was feared, for it suggested a new centre of worship if not a new worship as well, so the army assembled and made ready to go to war with their brethren whom they judged to have departed from the Lord and from His centre at Shiloh. Before joining in battle they were wise enough to send Phinehas, together with ten princes, one from each tribe, to investigate the situation and to learn exactly what they were up to in building such a great structure. To these envoys it appeared to be bordering on idolatry, and an introduction into the Nation of that which would bring down upon all the people the wrath of God.

When the deputation reached the eastern army there was nothing mild about its approach, for Phinehas and his princes spoke in stern terms, nor was there any evidence of conciliatory words in what they said. Without waiting for any explanation, or any excuse, they charged home to the supposed offenders the seriousness of what they had done, and branded it as rebellion so vile as to be comparable to the dreadful sin of Peor, an evil which they all knew was the most costly of all the failings of the desert. Being convinced of the oneness of the Nation, they could see only that the corruption in one part would be charged to all, so those living on the west side of Jordan would suffer the consequences of this dreadful work, as well as those living on the east. Toward the end of the speech a few words were added which did soften the matter, for they offered to allow the returned army and the tribes they represented an inheritance on the west side of the river, if this would solve the problem. A final warning concerning the seriousness of sin in the camp was given by a reference to the evil of Achan, which resulted in his own death and those of others with him.

In spite of the stern words spoken and heard, the reply of the tribes which had built the altar was both gentle and reasonable. They humbly agreed that if they were guilty of any of the alleged faults they deserved the judgment of God and the wrath of the Nation. They even avowed that their motive in building the altar was the very opposite of what had been suspected. Rather had it been built to prevent later generations concluding that, because the river separated the two parts of the Nation, each would have its own religious beliefs. This structure was erected to be a witness for all time that the Lord of the western people was the Lord of the eastern people. No thought of it being a substitute for the altar of the Lord, or of it being used for offerings, ever entered the builders' minds. When Phinehas heard their explanation, he, and those who accompanied him, were satisfied that what they gravely feared was not actually true. They returned to the camp at Shiloh and reported their findings to the satisfaction of all concerned, so they blessed God and gave up the idea of going to war with their brethren.

Few passages in the OT have so many lessons for assembly life as the verses we are considering. The story is strange, for this reason that in it there is no reference to Joshua, so it is an example of how the Nation would act in his absence. He apparently retired after he dismissed that part of the army which belonged to the tribes which settled on the east of Jordan. In this respect it illustrates for us some of the doings of the saints during the Lord's absence. One thing it makes clear is that if something is introduced for which we have no guidance from God it will ever rouse suspicion in the minds of the faithful. In the religious world to-day many things have been introduced that are foreign to the NT teaching. Whatever be the excuses made for them, the fact remains they have no warrant in Holy Scripture.

We see by the serious view taken of this altar that the faithful in Israel were not slack to curb any departure from the Lord that may arise. We must ever appreciate zeal for God, especially as so much evil is allowed to develop as the result of carelessness. There is always the danger, however, that our zeal may outstrip our wisdom. Rashness and impetuosity are not to be confused with courage and sound judgment. We shudder to think of what would have been the outcome had the army marched over the river and commenced slaughtering their brethren, men who had so recently risked their lives for their benefit, and helped them to obtain their inheritance. The redeeming feature of the case was that Phinehas and the princes investigated the matter before any such action was taken.

Another lesson of our passage is the great danger of acting upon suspicion. Something may look very like what we assume it to be, but on closer investigation it may turn out to be quite different. The western tribes were almost sure that they had discovered a grave departure from the Lord, but their fears proved to be groundless.

The example of Phinehas in speaking to supposed

offenders leaves much to be desired, nevertheless there was great frankness in his words, so those to whom they were spoken knew exactly how their actions had been viewed by him. When dealing with the wrongs of others we must be careful to make clear to them what their offences are. Most honest people like straight talking even when it hurts and give credit to those who speak it.

The answer given to the envoy by the supposed offenders was admirable, for it was a humble acknowledgment that, if the sin were as imagined, then the judgment on it was right and proper. The idea put forth that there was an attempt to set up a rival worship had never been entertained, but the whole scheme was designed to prevent such a thing taking place. Both sides could see that because the river split the Land into two parts there was a potential danger that the Nation would become divided in its worship. The acceptance of this explanation by Phinehas and his fellows shows the fairness of their minds, and proves that in spite of the sternness of their approach, they were humble enough to accept that they were wrong in their assumption.

The oneness of the Nation is another principle stressed in this story. Though living on different sides of Jordan, they were nonetheless one people. This is a major point in the attempt to set right what was thought to be wrong. Throughout the story, the evil of any part of the Nation is viewed as having dire consequences for the whole of it. While the figure of the one body is not here, yet the principle of its unity is here seen. The two cases sighted, those of Peor and Achan, had taught the people that the sin of one, or of a few, can bring down God's wrath upon the whole congregation. The same principle operates in an assembly, for if one member suffers, all the other members suffer with it. Likewise, if one sins, the whole company shares in the shame of it.

We cannot help but notice the change in the minds of the congregation at Shiloh. When Phinehas left they were preparing for war and when he returned and reported the true story they were blessing God. None was complaining that he had been too soft, nor did any say that time will tell whether or not the goodly words spoken by the supposed offenders were sincere. We ought to be deeply thankful to God if evils which have been rumoured did not occur, and that when we assumed such to be true we were proved to be wrong.

JOSHUA'S FAREWELL MESSAGES (23:1-24:28)

Apparently Joshua, after he had dismissed the army of the two tribes and half tribe, slipped into retirement and lived in the enjoyment of his inheritance in Mount Ephraim. Exactly how long the period was which elapsed between his dismissal of the army and his summons of the elders is difficult to determine, but possibly some twenty years of the closing part of his life were spent in this way. We have noticed that he was not engaged in the affairs of the Nation, so he most likely kept in the background and enjoyed his well-earned rest. When his end was approaching, however, he had, like Moses before him, a deep concern for those he was leaving behind. In these two chapters we have his parting words, in which he expresses his fears for the people, and gives them counsel. We can well understand his burden, for he had the honour of leading them into their possessions, he had been with them since they left Egypt, and they had become dear unto him. The time has now come when he must leave them, so the great general of the battlefield is no longer wielding his sword, but instead is using his tongue, and preaching, as it were, his two final sermons. The former was delivered to the representatives of the congregation, possibly near to his home in Mount Ephraim, and the latter was preached at Shechem. Some have thought that the expression here used, "before God" implies the presence of the Ark and the Tabernacle, and that these had been removed on this occasion from Shiloh. However, this may not be what is intended, but rather a simple reminder that God was present and would hear all that was being said. In the former address he reminded the people of what the Lord had done for them, and promised them that if they loved Him and obeyed Him He would continue to help them, but that if they turned away from Him He would forsake them. In the latter, he rehearsed the history of the people from the days of Abraham until their present position. He challenged them to serve the Lord, and finally raised up a great stone as a witness that they had chosen the Lord to be their God.

Already in ch. 13:1 we have been told that Joshua was old, but here the additional words "stricken in age" are added and may suggest that his life was all but over. He was not spared to be as old as Moses, but nevertheless, in spite of all he had passed through, he had been granted by God a long lifetime. Possibly few of his early contemporaries were alive at this time. Though his years were well over the century, yet his mind was clear, and his concern for the Nation as great as ever. Neither the rigours of the desert nor the strain of warfare had impaired his understanding, but all the past was as vivid in his memory as though it had recently happened. We might wonder that he did not remain at the helm, and that he, as an experienced captain, did not continue to steer the affairs of government. The answer lies in the fact that he knew his work was that of a warrior, so when the battles were over he retired into the background and allowed others to take over the running of the state. Many men have ruined their closing days by holding on to power long after their usefulness was passed. There are two dangers, one of going on too long, the other of retiring before the time. It is interesting to contrast his early days, when he was a slave in the brick-yards of Egypt, with these closing twenty years in the enjoyment of the Land of milk and honey. Moses had no such favour, but was in harness until the last day. Although during these years Joshua was not actively engaged in the running of the affairs of the Nation, he was deeply concerned about its welfare, and especially as to how it would be preserved when he would be no longer with it. No doubt this was his motive in calling the leaders to him, for he knew, as we all do, that parting words can be weighty, and are often rehearsed, and stay in the memory long after other words are forgotten. Examples of the importance of this abound in Scripture. Jacob's dying song, the song of Moses in Deuteronomy, the last words of David, the upper-room ministry of Christ, and Paul's final letter are samples which come to mind.

There could have been a temptation for Israel to imagine that all the victories of the past few years were won by their own strength and military skill, but Joshua reminds them that it was the Lord who fought for them. They had only to recall the fall of the walls of Jericho and the various encounters with the great kings, to be convinced that nothing of their own qualities could have accomplished so much. What had been done in Canaan must have been the wonder of that age, and the talk of the then known world. The mighty God of Jacob had made His name known to that generation in a way seldom witnessed hitherto. For any people to have ventured into that Land without divine help would have been not only dangerous but suicidal. From Jordan to the Great Sea the battle had raged and the spoils had been gathered, so that the down-trodden people had become not only owners of Land but possessors of incalculable wealth. Not that there were no enemies left, for the inhabitants were there by their thousands, and could only be driven out gradually, for, as explained in Deut 7:22 if they had been destroyed all at once, then the wild beasts would have swarmed the Land. There was still fighting to be done, and fresh opportunities for the new generation to prove the power of the God of their fathers.

The first exhortation Joshua gave to the leaders reminds us of His own commission mentioned in ch. 1. There he was instructed to be very courageous in obeying the commandments of the Law, so here he in turn enjoins them to do just this. They were not to divert from these in any direction, neither were they to mingle with the heathen who, at least for a time, would be dwelling beside them. Neither were they to use the names of the false gods worshipped by the Canaanites, nor indeed were they even to be mentioned among themselves. Thus the two vital principles, obedience and separation, were pressed upon them, and explained as the secret of future success. We have only to read the Book of Judges to learn the importance of these two injunctions. Throughout its pages it is patent that the neglect of them led to defeat and bondage. The promise is added, "one man of you shall chase a thousand: for the Lord your God is he that fighteth for you, as he hath promised you", so they had every reason and encouragement to keep right with the Lord, for He is a "man of war", and the One who would enable them to possess the entire Land. In order to enjoy His great power they must realise the importance of loving Him. This is the secret which would enable them to submit to His claims, for a devoted heart will count it a pleasure to obey His word, and at the same time will be careful not to put any one or any object in His place. The Lord Himself said, "If ye love me, ye will keep my commandments" (John 14:15 RV). Obviously Joshua knew that the passing of time would make life very difficult for the people, because there was the ever present danger that contact with the inhabitants of the Land could readily develop into friendship, and when this would continue for a time, it could blind the minds of the Israelites to the seriousness of idolatry. We know that later they disobeyed God and intermarried with the heathen. Likewise we know that the curse of the Nation was that it so readily turned to idols, and sank to the lowest depths of the practices of idolaters. Thus the warnings did not concern an imaginary danger unlikely to ever happen, but were prophetic in the sense that the evils here mentioned did actually occur later, to the downfall of those involved.

In order to deter them from trifling with this serious matter, he spelled out to them in no uncertain terms the punishment they would endure if they departed from the Lord. First, the enemy would no longer be driven out; secondly, they would be snared and trapped in the bondage that idolatry inevitably brings with it; thirdly, they would have to bear the painful scourge of abuse, together with the even more painful pricks of thorns in the eyes; and fourthly, they would, under God's judgments, perish from off the good Land which they were meant to possess. With such faithful warnings ringing in their ears from their dying leader, we are not surprised that the elders which outlived Joshua were preserved from departure, but we are amazed at the apostasy which occurred in the second generation. Only by neglecting this stern and faithful ministry could they have dared to turn aside as they did.

In these injunctions we detect a close resemblance to the words of Moses in Deuteronomy. In ch. 31:28 he had gathered together the elders, just as Joshua did here. The unusual word used by Joshua, translated "expel" in v. 5, which means "thrust out", is taken from Deut 11:23, and the expression, "turn not aside therefrom to the right hand or to the left" is from Deut 5:32 and 28:14. The danger of mixing with the nations around is stressed in Deut 7:2 - 4, and the warning that intercourse with them would bring a snare is given in v. 16. The idea of cleaving to the Lord occurs in Deut 10:20; 11:22, and the warning that departure from Him would mean that the curses which were on the heathen would fall upon themselves, occurs in Deut 28:15. Thus we can see that the parting words of Moses had sunk down into the heart of his servant, and that the ministry given some twenty-seven years earlier was still needed, and is here repeated. Both leaders detected certain tendencies and weaknesses in the people which they led, so both felt the need to warn them so strongly against these dangers. Neither the passage of time nor the exciting experiences in the Land had changed their hearts, so now that they were more exposed to temptation, by being closer to idolatry, the warnings were even more needful than when they were first given by Moses in the wilderness.

It was a joy to Joshua to realise that nothing had failed of all the lavish promises given him by God; all had been fulfilled. However, there is another side to this, for if God is faithful to keep all His promises of good, it follows that He will not be slack in carrying out all the threats of punishment for disobedience which He has made. In a sense the Israelites were just tenants in the Land, and God was its owner. He had evicted the original tenants because of their evil ways, so, if in the course of time the favoured people begin to practise the sins of the Canaanites, they are assured that they too will be evicted. We cannot help but notice that each time the "Land" is mentioned by Joshua in these verses he calls it "good Land". He would emphasise its quality, so that they would value it all the more.

When we turn to the second and final gathering of the people and Joshua's closing message to them (ch. 24:1 - 28), we may wonder why it was not delivered at Shiloh, which was the chosen place for the Tabernacle at that time. However, Shechem was one of those sacred spots in the Land which had treasured memories for them, for it was at Shechem that Abraham the father of the Nation first built an altar, after he had received his first promise from the Lord at the time when he entered Canaan (Gen 12:6, 7). Furthermore, it was at this place that the covenant was established by Joshua when he erected an altar of whole stones and wrote on them a copy of the law of Moses, and afterwards read all the words of the law with its blessings and curses (ch. 8:30 - 35). Perhaps also the fact that at Shechem Jacob cleansed his house from idolatry had some influence in the choice of it as a suitable venue for this solemn occasion. In this address we have two main thoughts. First, a rehearsal of God's goodness from the call of Abraham until that day (vv. 1 - 13); and secondly, because of this, the people should serve the Lord and renounce all idolatry (vv. 14 - 25).

Joshua began his address with, "Thus saith the God of Israel", and so impresses upon his audience the authority for what he is about to say and the responsibility involved for those who were listening. He turned their minds back to the origin of the Nation, and to the time when Abraham their father lived on the other side of the

River (Euphrates), and reminded them that at that time the family were all idolaters. The favour of God was revealed in that He called Abraham from this centre of idolatry, and brought him into the Land of Canaan. The patriarch not only left his father's house, but left his father's gods, never to return to either again. For thirty years he moved through his new country under the hand of God, and then an additional favour was granted to him in the birth of Isaac. He spent another sixty years before he saw his grandchildren born, who were named Jacob and Esau. The latter possessed his inheritance in Mount Seir, and did so long before his brother entered into his portion. Joshua proceeded to trace the history of Jacob from the going into Egypt until the great deliverance by the hand of Moses. He was not in the company of those who went down into Egypt, but he was amongst those who sang at the victory over Pharaoh, and saw the latter being drowned in the Red Sea. Perhaps he had vivid memories of the rattling of the chariots, of the prancing of the horses as the host of the Egyptians drew near, and of the camp of Israel trembling at their approach. Well could he remember the boon which the Lord granted in the cloud of darkness which halted the advance of the enemy, and at the same time illuminated the path of the pursued.

The wanderings in the wilderness were passed over in the briefest possible way, even though throughout the forty years spent there the Israelites experienced many mercies and kindnesses from the Lord. The singular victories enjoyed on the east side of Jordan were specially dwelt upon, as they were the beginnings of the conquests which were more especially, and more recently, seen in Canaan. Joshua introduced Balaam into his message, for he was the supreme sample of one who had power with his gods. The Lord again showed His favour to His people in that He turned the curse of the false prophet into a blessing. Of all the conquered cities in the Land, only one was mentioned - Jericho. It was the grand sample of what the Lord did to all the rest as He led His people into their possessions. The one feature which marked the taking of this fortified city was the absence of any skill or war effort on the part of the besiegers. They could take no credit for the collapsing of its walls, nor did any weapon, such as sword and bow so common in general warfare, play any part in their fall.

The final point raised in this historic survey was the favour granted to the Israelites in giving them such a good Land. They were not only helped by the Lord to destroy the defences of the enemies, but were enabled by Him to take possession of their treasures. They were not given a waste or barren wilderness, but a Land filled with houses and ready for occupation, so they had no need to toil in order to erect their dwellings, but simply to walk into them and occupy what others had built. They could not live in these dwellings without supplies of food, so they ate of the corn which had grown on the cultivated fields. They were not only given the necessities of life, but with these they enjoyed the luxuries of wine and oil which the vineyards and olive yards produced. Unlike settlers in many new countries, who have to clear away the shrubbery or trees and then toil to break up the soil and make it ready for planting, they inherited a Land where all this was already done. They had no need to wait for years to obtain the crops of fruit, for the orchards were in full production.

We cannot help noticing the vast change which had taken place in the Land since the days of Abraham. Apparently in his time one could wander from one end of the Land to the other without coming to any large settlement or city. He was never confronted with fortified cities, or with those who were competing for possession of any particular part of the Land. He must have cultivated wheat, or else some of his neighbours did so and he purchased it from them, for he baked bread. We know that Isaac sowed grain and reaped a good harvest, but the main occupation of the patriarchs was shepherding sheep and herding cattle. Just as Israel developed while in Egypt into a Nation of over two million, so too the population of Canaan must have increased dramatically during the same period. In more recent times the same phenomenon has occurred in America and parts of Canada.

There are a number of places in the Scripture where the history of the God's earthly people is recalled in some detail. In Neh 9 the Levites, while confessing the departure from God which brought the Nation into Babylon, went over the past, and owned that the God who created all things, chose Abraham and his posterity, and made a covenant with him. His seed, alas! turned away from their father's God, and eventually were swept off the Land and taken to Babylon. In Ps 105 and 106 the same history is retold. In the former the faithfulness of God is demonstrated, and in the latter the unfaithfulness of His people. Stephen, in his defence before the council, again covers the same story, but brings it up to date by showing the culmination of the faithlessness of Israel in the rejection of Christ. In each of these historical reviews there is a different purpose. When Joshua was telling the story of the past, he was doing so in order to stress how that the God of Israel was far above every other false god who was worshipped by man. Had Abraham's fathers worshipped one as great as the Lord, he would never have abandoned Him. Had the gods of Egypt been superior to the Lord, then the plagues in Egypt and the drowning of the host at the Red Sea would never have occurred. Had the gods of the Canaanites been what they thought them to be, then the victories of Joshua would have been impossible. In this reasoning, he was showing the people why he had chosen the Lord to be his God, and demonstrating to them the folly of turning away to idolatry. When the Psalms were written, they were intended to produce praise from the hearts of the singers, when they recounted the Lord's wonderful kindness to them, and also to call to mind, that in spite of the Nation's unfaithfulness and departure, He still remembered His covenant, and showed, because of it, His tender mercies. The purpose Stephen had in his account of the same history was to show that all the deliverers God sent to Israel were rejected. Whether it was Joseph, Moses, or even Christ, all suffered the same treatment, so the people most privileged were destitute of the ability to discern who were their benefactors, and therefore despised all of them.

Having proved the superiority of the God of Israel, Joshua pressed home his challenge. If this God is all that He has proved Himself to be, then fear Him and put away all idols, but if any want to go back to the ancient idols that were worshipped in Ur or the idols which were worshipped by the nations around them, then the choice is his to make. Joshua himself had no hesitation as to what he would do, for already he had made up his mind to serve the Lord. Obviously the people had more confidence in themselves as regards their faithfulness than had Joshua. Still, they protested that they would never forsake the Lord, for He had delivered them from Egypt, and had given them the Land which they now occupied.

It seems strange, in spite of the bold confession of the people concerning their service of the Lord, that Joshua would say to them, "Ye cannot serve the Lord".

What apparently he had in mind was, that His character is such that for a people to serve Him they must be holy as He is, and if they deviate from Him, as they were likely to do, then, because He is a jealous God He will not tolerate any rival, and so will fall upon them in His wrath. The strong language used here is meant to give them some idea of the seriousness of what they were promising. We have to realise that when Israel later turned to idolatry there was still the idea in their hearts that they believed in the Lord. In other words, they retained some relation to the Lord, but shared their worship of Him with other gods. Such mixture and confusion could never escape the judgment of the Lord. There was no thought in the minds of the people that they would ever turn away from the Lord, but they were poor judges of their own hearts. At the giving of the Law they manifested the same spirit, for they said, "All that the Lord hath spoken we will do" (Ex 19:8), yet before Moses returned from the mount they had turned to idolatry. On this occasion Joshua accepted the sincerity of the people, which had been firmly tested by what he had said to them, and this brought the meeting to the conclusion he had intended it to reach, so then he made a fresh covenant with the people there at Shechem. This solemn agreement entailed the determination of the people that they would have no other god but the Lord, and that they would serve Him only. To their credit, they did fulfil this agreement, for according to Judges 2:7 "The people served the Lord all the days of Joshua, and all the days of the elders that outlived Joshua", so his faithfulness was fruitful even after he was dead.

However difficult it may be for us to accept the fact, it does appear that Joshua deemed there were idols in the host of Israel. We know that throughout the wilderness journey idols had a place in some of their tents. Just as Jacob when at Shechem demanded that all idols in his tent should be buried under the oak tree, so Joshua, in the same place, makes the same demand. Indeed some imagine that the tree referred to later in the chapter was the same tree as was there in Jacob's day. The propensity to harbour idols seems never to have left the Nation, not even in its best days. Little wonder so much space in the OT is occupied in condemning them.

These two addresses of Joshua have a host of lessons in them, especially for those who have a care for the saints and are about to leave them. Uppermost in the minds of such should be, and usually is, the importance of obedience to the word of God. Those longest in the school of God learn that every departure from the teaching of Scripture is more costly than might at first be estimated. Obedience requires courage, and at times can be fulfilled only at great cost, but disobedience has such dire results that no estimate can be fully made of its sad consequences. The confusion in the religious world is a patent example of what is produced when the word of God is set aside. Another principle appearing in Joshua's message is the necessity to keep separate from the world, especially in its social and its religious activities. He was aware that if there were intermingling in the domestic sphere, there would soon be intermingling in the religious realm. Leaders cannot take those they lead out of the world, for the Lord Himself would not pray that this should be so, but they can do their best to warn and instruct the saints of the danger it presents to them, and the subtlety of its allurements. Nothing has been more harmful to assembly testimony than the attempts which have been made by some leaders to cater for the flesh by introducing sports and games to entertain the young, even going so far at times as to have the unsaved mixing in these activities.

Saints need encouragement as well as warnings, so we can learn from Joshua how to bring to their minds the Lord's doings for them in the past, and very especially what He is prepared to do, not only for them, but through them. "One man of you shall chase a thousand" were words charged with power. There is ever the danger that they under-estimate the strength that is at their disposal when the Lord is with them. Elders have to be careful that their ministry is balanced, otherwise those who listen to them will become disheartened, and treat it and them as something which must be endured. If the word of God is to be obeyed and the world is to be shunned, then there must be more than mere instruction involved, so this leads us to see that this great man points out another essential for the people, namely, love to the Lord. The value of devotion of heart cannot be over-estimated. Where it is lacking there is little likelihood of either obedience or separation being practised.

Whether we think of these parting words of Joshua, or of the closing words of John in his epistle, "Little children keep yourselves from idols", we see that mature men of God become painfully aware of the seriousness of idolatry. Brethren in responsibility have no need in many parts of the world to warn the saints concerning the evil of bowing down to images made from wood or stone, but they have to stress in their ministry that, according to Paul, "Covetousness is idolatry" (Col 3:5), so they need to explain that one can be guilty of idolatry without having any tangible object before him. They must never forget the fact that anything which displaces the Lord in the heart is an idol.

The penalty Israel had to pay for departure from God was the loss of the good Land. This corresponds to the loss the saints experience when they drift away from the Lord. Our inheritance is a spiritual one, and is enjoyed in the soul and spirit. When the portion which is ours in Christ is apprehended and in measure surveyed, then the world becomes very small and its attractions lose their lustre, but if our hearts grown cold we cannot expect to enjoy our heavenly portion, so we become spiritually poor. Every true shepherd of the saints grieves if any for whom he cares has become entangled with earthly things and is no longer delighting his soul in the unsearchable riches of Christ, which are intended to be his portion. No true Israelite was happy when away from his Land, but was like those sitting by the rivers of Babylon, who hung their harps upon the willows and refused to sing. Likewise, it must be remembered that none really saved is happy while away from his spiritual inheritance.

The art of making the best use of past history is one which every leader should seek to learn. He has an inexhaustible store of inspired records in both Testaments. Like Joshua, he can use these to show the saints the wonders of their Lord, and the might of His power. Seldom does any matter arise in the assembly, but some example can be adduced from these, which has a bearing on it. The same is true of our personal lives, for many can testify that when in certain circumstances, which they thought were unique, they discovered in the Scriptures that others had trodden the same path before they were born. Paul, who was an outstanding leader, constantly taught the saints the lessons they should learn from their own conversion. He himself seldom preached or wrote without making some reference to his own experience on the Damascus Road. In a masterly way he used the failings of Israel in the wilderness to teach the Corinthians the seriousness of lusting after evil things, and to warn them to flee from idolatry (1 Cor 10). Even in his parting address to the elders (Acts 20), which in measure resembles Joshua's closing message here, more than half of it is occupied with his own past history. The heart of Joshua could find no greater joy in the elders before him, than to know that they had the same thoughts of the Lord as he had, and similarly Paul would fain produce in the elders before him the characteristics of his own life. Neither man had to apologise for past blunders, nor had either to say, "follow me, but not when I wandered away".

When the covenant was agreed and the Lord had been chosen as the only One to serve, then Joshua wrote this down in the book of the law so that the record of it could be brought forth as a witness of what was then confirmed. He was likely given a copy of the law by Moses, and now he adds to it this important postscript. We have noted that he had changed from using the sword to the use of the tongue, and now with the pen he is here seen as a scribe. Not only was this covenant preserved in writing, but a memorial of it, in the form of a great stone, was placed under an oak tree. We have noted many such monuments throughout this book, but this is the last of them, and one of the most important. This tree is said to be in the sanctuary of God, but this does not mean it was in the Tabernacle, but rather that it was in the place where the Lord's presence was realised, and where a sacred vow was taken. There can be little doubt that at this time, the thoughts of what Jacob did at the same place were before Joshua's mind. It will be recalled that at Shechem the patriarch had buried the idols of his household under an oak. Some have imagined that here was the same tree still standing and testifying to the same truth. While this may not be so, yet what was here erected would be a witness to future generations of the covenant made before God, that He alone would be served in Israel.

THE DEATH AND BURIAL OF JOSHUA (24:29-31)

With all his responsibilities discharged and his final messages to the nation delivered, it was no embarrassment for Joshua to go, as he said, "the way of all the earth". He had reached the ripe age of one hundred and ten years, so was spared as long as his great ancestor, Joseph, who also died at this age. He was buried on the slopes of one of the hills near to his home in Ephraim where he had his inheritance. The loss to Israel in his departure could never be measured, but he had served his own generation and had done it well. In spite of the changing circumstances and the many temptations which crossed his path, he finished without a blot on his character or a charge laid against him. He left behind a legacy, not of material wealth, but of a good example for those coming after him to follow. His influence remained long after he was gone, for the generation which knew him were so impressed by his manner of life that they also served the Lord. Like Moses, he had no son to take his place, nor did he arrange for a successor. Doubtless he was mourned by all who knew him, but for some unknown reason there is no mention of this in the passage. Possibly his long period of retirement meant that he had faded from the limelight, so, in a sense, he was somewhat out of the minds of the people by the time his death took place. Few men experience so many changes in life as he did, for he was a slave in Egypt, a soldier in the wilderness and in the Land, a spy in enemy territory, and a servant of the Lord.

THE BONES OF JOSEPH BURIED (24:32)

Another grave was opened in Shechem in which were interred the bones of Joseph. Whether they were laid to rest some time before this or not we do not know, but it is fitting that the mention of his funeral should be inserted at this point, for Joshua was a descendant of his. At his death, he had prophesied that Israel would be delivered from Egypt, and asked that they would carry up his bones and bury them in the land of his fathers. All his brothers and his father were buried in Canaan, so he too desired to lie there. Though much failure marked the Nation in the wilderness, and many who began the journey from Egypt were buried in the desert, yet these bones were so treasured that they were never lost or destroyed. Not until the land had been captured and the site of the grave secured could this interment be possible. Hundreds of years passed by from the time Jacob purchased this plot from the children of Hamor and bequeathed it to Joseph, and many had used the land over these centuries who never thought of its rightful owner, but now it is not only in the hands of the original owner's descendants, but is being used for a most honourable purpose. In the burial of these bones we see that the Israelites recognised the truth of Gen 3:19, "for dust thou art, and unto dust shalt thou return". They could have continued to allow the bones to remain in the coffin and left them unburied but they did not do so. Perhaps this was better for the people may have made them an object of worship as they did with the brazen serpent. Few, if any, have been so long dead before being buried. Perhaps this is why the bones are mentioned instead of the body. He was embalmed in Egypt, and this may have meant that his body would have been preserved, but no hint of this is given in this verse.

THE DEATH AND BURIAL OF ELEAZER (24:33)

Another funeral is mentioned which also was to Mount Ephraim, it was that of Eleazar the priest. He was a contemporary of Joshua's, and knew the toiling in Egypt, the trials of the wilderness, and the triumphs in the Land. He had the strange experience of being with Moses, who stripped off from his father, Aaron, the high-priestly robes and put then them upon him. As soon as this was done, his father fell dead at their feet. Unlike both Moses and Joshua, Eleazar was succeeded by his son, Phinehas, who carried on the high-priestly office, and had his inheritance in Mount Ephraim where he buried his father.

The three great men brought together in these verses, likely because they were all buried in Mount Ephraim, were very different in their calling. Joseph was a wise administrator in the palace of Pharaoh, Joshua was a captain in the army, and Eleazar was the anointed high-priest. Each of them is typical of the Lord Himself. The time is coming when He will gird the sword on His thigh and subdue His enemies as did Joshua. He like Joseph will prove to be a wise administrator in His kingdom, when He shall have dominion throughout the universe, and He, like Eleazar, will be a priest upon His throne. Already He is High-priest in heaven, but His priesthood will continue throughout His reign, and forever.

Most likely none of these men ever thought that his experiences and doings would prove to be of a typical nature, nor did any of them realise that some of the features of Christ were produced in him by God's power and grace. As we read their histories we can discern these features, and compare them with the Gospel records of Christ. They were being allowed to pass through life and find in it much that would foreshadow His course. The highest honour God can confer on any mortal is to make him wear features of His own Son. Most of our experiences are designed, by divine grace, to bring this transformation about. The more the ungodly go on in their evil ways, the more like the devil they become, but the more men live in fellowship with God, the more they become like Him in their ways. Full conformity, however, awaits the Lord's coming, when "we shall be like him, for we shall see him as he is" (1 John 3:2).

APPENDIX

SOME STRANGE FEATURES OF THE BOOK OF JOSHUA

NO REBELLION OF THE PEOPLE

There are some elements which we would expect in this book, which are noticeably absent. Some of these we have mentioned in the course of our writing, but we will now point them out more distinctly. Perhaps the most surprising to our minds is that throughout its pages there is not the slightest sign of rebellion or quarrelling amongst the people. When Moses was leading them, they had his heart broken time and time again. At almost every juncture in the wilderness they were either murmuring or threatening to return to Egypt. On at least one occasion they were ready to stone him. One would be tempted to ask, "Are these the same people who are being led by Joshua? What has changed their way and manners?" It cannot be that Joshua was a leader superior to his master, nor can it be that he was held in higher respect by them. Whatever honours the former deserved, and these were many, yet the latter had an intimacy with the Lord second to none, and was one of Israel's greatest sons. Furthermore, it is said of Moses that he was the meekest man in all the earth, so he was not in trouble with the people because of any twist in his character, or because he was a difficult man with whom to work. Even when the Land was being distributed, and each had his portion allotted, to our surprise there was no quarrelling, for all know that in allocating anything that is varied in content, it is almost impossible to satisfy everyone who obtains his share. When the seven tribes saw how small their territories were, compared with the choice portions already allotted to Judah and Ephraim, we might well expect there would have been some loud complaining, but not so, neither did these two highly favoured tribes complain when some of the territory already given to them was taken away and given to other tribes.

What brought about this remarkable change? There are a number of factors which had a bearing on it. One of these was, that the Nation was thrilled with the success, not only in crossing Jordan, but in the early victories granted on its other side. When all is going well, and goals are being reached, most seem to forget the hardship involved in gaining them, but if failure dogs the path, and disappointment confronts at every turn, then tempers become frayed, and complaints flow freely. Another factor which played a part in this change of conduct was, that the new generation, which was reared in the wilderness, had witnessed the consequences of rebellion, and therefore dreaded any such disaster befalling themselves. The dead bodies which were strewn over the wilderness must have spoken loudly to their hearts, and told them plainly that their God will not tolerate murmuring, especially in His own people. Perhaps being in the land of their fathers, and seeing all the places which they had heard others speak about, was another factor which had a calming effect upon their spirits. Their respect for Abraham must have caused them to feel it a great privilege to tread the ground where he had trodden, and to graze their sheep and cattle on the very hills where his flocks had fed.

In assembly life, we find that if the work of God is prospering, souls being saved in Gospel efforts, and the ministry to the saints bearing fruit in their lives, then complaining is reduced to a minimum, but if failure and barrenness prevail, then fault is found with the leadership, and the blame for it laid at its door. The tendency to ignore the fact that the cause for failure could lie with the entire company, or the thought that it could be allowed by the Lord as a time of testing for the saints, is banished out of the minds of most. Though not literally passing through an earthly desert, both the individual believer and the gathered companies have wilderness experiences. In these their weaknesses come to the surface and give cause for humility and exercise, but care is needed, lest the blame for such dark days is not wrongly attached to the leadership.

THE HIGH WALLS AND THE GIANTS

When the spies returned to Moses, the most daunting features of the Land they had surveyed were its high walls and its tall giants. The former they hyperbolically stated were up to heaven, and in like manner they described the latter as making themselves appear like grasshoppers in comparison. We would expect that these two obstacles in the way of their advancement would be much to the fore in this book, but to our surprise no such feature marks it. Apart from Jericho, which had its walls miraculously dealt with, we would scarcely know if any other city in the Land was so fortified. We do not think Jericho was unique in this respect; other such places must have dotted the Land, yet no stress is laid upon the problem of overcoming them.

That there were giants in the various places captured is made clear, but again, there is no stress placed upon the difficulty they caused. The old man Caleb, was able to dislodge three of them from the city he took, and these seemed to give him no great concern. Either the grasshoppers had grown taller, or the giants had become ordinary men, or else the Lord strengthened His people so that no foe could resist them. The last we recognise as the truth. We know, of course that not all the giants, especially those of the Philistines, were destroyed until the time of David, nevertheless, some of them were slain during the conquest led by Joshua.

The lesson we can learn from this matter is, "That the clouds we so much dread, are big with mercy and can break, with blessings on our head". Much that to human reasoning looks impossible can easily be overcome with the Lord's help. We can exaggerate the difficulties, but we can never exaggerate the Lords power.

THE FEASTS OF THE LORD

In the Book of Joshua we are kept informed regarding the Tabernacle and where it was located, but strangely enough we have no mention of any of the feast days being kept by Israel, except the Passover in ch. 5. Possibly in a time of warfare there was no formal gathering to God's dwelling-place, but we would expect when the "land had rest" that the normal solemn assemblings would be resumed. Obviously the Tabernacle ritual under the high-priest was continued, and possibly use made of the Urim and Thummim, but beyond this we have no hint in the book of any sacrifices being offered at it. What is even more strange, is that when sacrifices were offered by Joshua, they were offered on the altar he built of stone and not on the brazen altar (ch. 8:31). As we have already seen, even His two closing messages were not delivered in the Tabernacle precincts, but in places some distance away. All this is different from the story of Moses in the wilderness, for at almost every crisis he stood at the Tabernacle and the cloud appeared which indicated that the Lord's presence was being specially granted for the occasion.

The answer to this apparent abnormality could be that the writer of this book, which records the conquering and possessing of the Land, had not, as part of his purpose, any thought of dealing with religious matters. Keeping warfare and worship apart may seem strange to us, but we ought to remember that our sanctuary experiences are in the calm of God's presence, and in the place where we enjoy the help of our Great High Priest. On the other hand, we all know that in our prayer life the enemy puts up fierce opposition, and can only be overcome by the exercise of faith. In Hebrews we learn that we have boldness to enter the worship, in Ephesians we are taught that we are in the heavenlies, and are viewed as wrestling with the powers of darkness, and needing to be clothed in the armour of God. In the former there are no weapons needed, in the latter there is no mention of the help of the High-Priest.

In worship the whole congregation was involved, but in the warring only those who were soldiers were employed. Ability, strength, and training were involved in being a good soldier, but the weakest of the people could bring his offering and present it to the Lord. Gift is required to preach the Gospel and to minister to the saints, but the most undeveloped brother can pour out his gratitude to God even though it be not couched in sublime language.

THE ABSENCE OF SINGING AND REJOICING

As soon as the Israelites crossed the Red-Sea they sang the song of Moses, but no such celebrations are to be found in the book of Joshua, not that there was nothing in its story about which to sing. Whether we think of the crossing of Jordan, or of the walls of Jericho falling down, or of the many victories which followed, we imagine that some evidence of appreciation would have appeared, that some emotions would have been stirred, and that some lips would have poured forth praise to God. We cannot help being amazed that neither the parting of the flooded waters, nor the crashing down of stout walls, seemed to arouse any excitement, but all passed as though nothing abnormal had taken place, and as though the miraculous was taken for granted. The answer to this question lies in the fact that in the book of Joshua the religious exercise of the people is kept in the background, for only on one occasion throughout its pages do we see Joshua on his face in prayer to God (ch. 7:6 - 9)

THE ARMY UNDER JOSHUA

Another feature of this book is the absence in it of any reference to the distinguished amongst the warriors. There is no list given of the mighty men, nor are there any captains of the army referred to as worthy of special honour. Except for the thirty six men who died at the first attempt to take Ai, there is no record in its pages of the loss of one Israelite in battle. Even in the most successful operations of present day warfare it is not unusual for some few lives to be lost, but in wars lasting for seven years it is most wonderful that all life was preserved.

However, we must remember that this was no ordinary conflict, but an execution of God's judgment on a corrupt society, so it was reasonable for Him to preserve the lives of those who were the executors of His purpose. Truly the battle was the Lord's, so no man could claim any glory for its success.

THE ENTRANCE INTO REST

One point is stressed throughout the book of Joshua which seems rather strange in the midst of its conflicts, it is the mention of rest. "The land rested from war" (ch. 11:23), "The land had rest from war" (ch. 14:15), "The Lord gave them rest round about" (ch. 21:41), "The Lord your God hath given rest unto your brethren" (ch. 22:4), and "The Lord hath given rest unto Israel" (ch. 23:1), are statements which we might expect to read in the history of the balmy days of Solomon's reign, but they do indeed appear to be out of keeping with this book. Perhaps the emphasis on rest is because the wanderings in the wilderness were passed, and the people were at length settled in a land which they could call their own. In one sense the wars were over and the enemy defeated, but in another sense the struggle to possess the inheritance and drive out the Canaanites was to continue, even after Joshua's death. Just as in Christian experience we obtained rest when we trusted Christ, but this has been followed by continuous exercise and conflict, so Joshua gave Israel rest yet they had still to fight for their possessions.

oooOooo